No Longer at Ease

Seven Churches and the Empire

A Study of Revelation 1-3

Kent J. Ulery

Cover Photo

This mosaic of John receiving and dictating Revelation to his scribe, Prochoros, graces the entrance to the Cave of the Apocalypse on Patmos.

ISBN: 146110212X
ISBN-13: 978-1461102120

…We returned to our places, these Kingdoms,
But no longer at ease here, in the old dispensation,
With an alien people clutching their gods…

— T.S. Elliot's *Journey of the Magi*

CONTENTS

FORWARD

This study is for congregations longing for quality curricula for an adult Bible study; prayer circles seeking an informed guide for difficult scriptures; pilgrims touring Turkey with itineraries including cities mentioned in Revelation; and all interested in exploring the timeless themes of good and evil, justice and power, spirituality and materialism from a Christian perspective.

While the author of Revelation clearly intended the work to be read by the church in every place and throughout time, he addresses seven specific first-century congregations in seven very different cities in the Roman province of Asia. This book focuses on the seven letters of the Risen Christ to those seven churches, found in the second and third chapters of Revelation.

We will review distinctive characteristics and historical events associated with each city, discuss daily life in the Roman Empire during the reign of Emperor Domitian, and examine the relationship between Christianity and Judaism. At the time of Revelation's writing, were they separate and distinct religious faiths, or was the first a protected subgroup of the second? We will acquaint ourselves with the style and symbols of apocalyptic writing, familiar to the author's original audience but foreign to us. We will learn the connotation of a few important Greek words and some subtleties of Greek grammar commonly lost in English translations. We will explore the land's topography and unearth the implications of archaeological findings. And we will be sensitive to a non-scientific worldview in which mysterious, unexplainable, and spiritual realities are embraced.

Majoring in metaphors, Revelation reads more like poetry than prose. The logic is not the linear reasoning of *A implies B implies C*; rather, the movement is cyclical – critical themes touched upon, returned to, and repeated again and again and again. To be read as much with our hearts as through our heads, our imaginations need freedom for Revelation's symbols and stories to do their work.

At the same time our imaginations need discipline to avoid flights of fanciful interpretation. We would discern the letters' implications for our contemporary time, but we cannot do so without first immersing ourselves in their original setting.

Finally, we will be praying for ears to hear (as each of the seven letters exhorts) what the Spirit is saying to the churches.

Intended to be read aloud, Revelation is oral speech penned for recitation before worshipping congregations. The language is classically rhetorical, employing persuasion's art and power – sometimes sounding as if we are in a court of law listening to the prosecution's case, sometimes ringing like a political debate in which an opponent's position is countered, and sometimes imploring with the ceremonial language of praise and blame.[1]

The ability of Revelation to change lives is unleashed when Christians gather as faith communities, listening for the word of God in words which, as Revelation puts it, are true and worthy of our trust. Accordingly, we suggest beginning and ending each session by reading the text aloud. The translations of the letters introducing each chapter are mine, with all other Biblical references taken from the *New Revised Standard Version*.[2] Since no translation perfectly captures the original language, we encourage you to read aloud from several translations.

Please join me in thanking:

- the late Professor Bruce Metzger, the gentle New Testament scholar at Princeton Theological Seminary, who first introduced me to the serious study of Revelation;

- the Michigan Conference of the United Church of Christ, which granted sabbatical leave for me to do research and writing, along with the opportunity to encounter the angels of numerous local congregations;

- the Haslett Community Church, United Church of Christ, in Haslett, Michigan; St. Paul Evangelical Lutheran Church of America in East Lansing, Michigan; Hope United Church of Christ in Frasier, Michigan; the Michigan Region of the Christian Church (Disciples of Christ); the United Northern Association of the Michigan Conference of the United Church of Christ; the Penn West

---

[1] Fiorenza, Elisabeth Schüssler. *Revelation: Vision of a Just World.* Minneapolis, Fortress Press, 1991. Pages 20-22.

[2] *NRSV.* © Division of Christian Education of the National Council of Churches of Christ in the United States of America, 1989.

Conference of the United of Christ; and the Great Lakes Regional United Church of Christ Staff Retreat – all of which opened their doors for me to test by teaching the earliest content of this study;

- United Church of Christ Conference Ministers Russ Mitman, Alan McLarty, and Sheldon Culver, who never missed a chance to ask if the book was done yet;

- the summer 2009 exegetical class on Revelation at Bangor Theological Seminary, whose probing queries turned into the discussion questions for each chapter;

- my wife, Meg, who listened to every word more than once, kept asking questions until I explained clearly, and constantly encourages my ministry through her love for the church and her concern for the world's hurting; and, most importantly,

- God, revealed in the Risen Christ, who through the Holy Spirit grants courage in the struggle for justice and peace.

1 INTRODUCTION

September 11, 2001. Al-Qaeda linked terrorists hijacked four passenger planes over the United States, intentionally flying two into the twin towers of the World Trade Center. The Pentagon was the target of the third airliner. Loaded with fuel for transcontinental destinations, these jets exploded upon collision, transformed into gigantic fiery bombs killing thousands. Thwarted was the mission of the fourth set of suicidal terrorists when the aircraft crashed in the Pennsylvania countryside, killing all on board.

Crowded around any available television, horrified by seeing the twin towers collapsing, Americans knew when the second plane hit we were not dealing with a tragic accident. When the third plane struck it became clear these were not random acts of violence. The terrorists' targets were selected for their symbolic value.

It was not any office building in New York City; it was the World Trade Center, the tallest set of buildings in America, the towering symbol of the global economic reach of the richest nation on earth.

It was not any military installation; it was the Pentagon, the central headquarters of America's military establishment, the fortress symbol of the planet's only remaining superpower.

Where was the last plane headed? Camp David? The White House? The State Department? As in the Tom Clancy novel, could it have been the hallowed halls of Congress?[3] Surely it, too, was aimed at one of the symbols of America's worldwide political prowess.

---

[3] Clancy, Tom. *Executive Orders.* ©Jack Ryan Limited Partnership. Printed by New York: G. P. Putnam's Sons, 1996.

1

Concluded President of the United States, George W. Bush, the terrorist act on 9-11 was an attack on freedom.

In response the President declared war against terrorism, an extended war unlike any the American people had fought previously, what he called "the first war of the new millennium." In apocalyptic style the President called upon the world's nations to choose sides – join the coalition of countries intent on battling the terrorists and those harboring them, or be numbered among America's enemies. The President repeated often that America had no quarrel with either the religion of Islam or the Iraqi people. Rather (again in apocalyptic style) the President defined the battle as against the forces of evil, assuring the nation that God was on America's side. While Mr. Bush never publicly characterized the conflict as a "holy war," the first bombs dropped on those who had declared a *jihad* on the United States exploded on Sunday morning while the heartland of America was in church praying.

Several days later I drove my mother from the hospital to her new apartment in an assisted living complex. Tired from trekking with her walker from the parking lot to the entry, we stopped to rest in the lobby. Immediately a crowd of residents – all seniors, all women, all well traveled – gathered to welcome her home.

Mom lived in a beautiful facility. A pleasant gazebo and professional croquet court grace the front lawn. Lunch is served with fresh flowers and linen napkins. There are no unpleasant odors. The furniture shows no signs of wear. It is precisely the kind of place where people retire so that they and their families don't have to worry anymore.

Nevertheless, on this day mom's friends were troubled. The terrorist act and ensuing war were on their minds. As we sat in the vestibule, the first question to me was: "Do you believe this is the beginning of Armageddon?" I didn't. But I found it fascinating they chose an obscure passage from Revelation to express their fears.

Obscure? Yes. In the scriptures the word "Armageddon" only appears once, in a single verse where it reads: "And they assembled them at the place that in Hebrew is called Harmaggedon." Note the variant spelling. Is there one "g" in the name or two? Two "d's" or just one? Does it actually begin with an "A" or should that first letter be an "H"? The earliest manuscripts of Revelation are inconsistent. No one knows how the word is spelled, the root meaning of the name, or where the city was, is, or shall be located.

Consult the commentaries and you are likely to read the name means "The Mountain of Megiddo." Located at the critical pass into the Holy Land's fertile central plain, Megiddo was the site of several important ancient battles.

Among the oldest verses in the Bible is Deborah's jubilant victory song over the defeated Canaanites by "the waters of Megiddo." Celebrating the end of twenty years of oppression, she sings of the overthrow of an army of nine hundred chariots of iron by the motley militia under her command.

Gideon's vastly outnumbered troops defeat the Midianites at Megiddo, thereby ending the annual incursion of camelback raiders intent on stealing the harvest from across the Jordan. That legendary victory is so against odds, so obviously miraculous, that the biblical storyteller gives God all the credit.

During the evil reign of King Ahab and Queen Jezebel, the prophet Elijah builds an altar near Megiddo on Mount Carmel, piles wood upon it, and soaks the wood with gallons of water. When God sends fire from heaven to consume the offering, it settles the question of whether Yahweh or Baal is the true God.

More than a century after it happened, the people still mourn the untimely death of Judah's young reformer-king, Josiah, killed in the struggle against Pharaoh Neco at Megiddo.

Given that battles of such magnitude in Israel's history were fought there, conclude several commentators, where else would the author of Revelation be referring than to "The Mountain of Megiddo" as the site for the last and most decisive battle in human history?

Accordingly millions of pilgrims journey to the Holy Land to see this mountain where the final conflict between good and evil, the ultimate match between God and Satan, the war to end history will be fought…only to discover there is no Mountain of Megiddo! Megiddo is located on the Plain of Jezreel.

While alternative theories regarding the spelling, meaning, and location of Armageddon vie for scholarly acceptance, mystery remains until we recognize Armageddon is not so much a physical place as a spiritual metaphor which affirms by faith that, no matter how great the evil of the moment, the ultimate victory belongs to God.

Confronted by so great a tragedy, people say life changed on September 11th. Certainly the suffering and death of so many left no doubt about the ferociousness of evil. Once the terrorists struck, many found themselves questioning the presence and power of God. Remember the quivering voices of those gathered in sanctuaries to pray?

Is God in control of the universe or not?

Is Christ truly the Lord of heaven and earth?

Is the Holy Spirit strong enough to override the forces of evil in our world?

These were the questions on the minds of the senior citizens in mom's complex when they raised the issue of Armageddon. They also are the questions at the heart of Revelation – a book which barely made it into the Bible and is ignored or misunderstood to this day.

Revelation most likely was written near the end of the first century during the last days of the Roman Emperor Domitian. However, its inclusion in the canon remained controversial for centuries. Three hundred years after being authored, Cyril of Jerusalem decreed Revelation should not be read in public or in private. Seven hundred years after being penned Revelation still was not on the list of scriptural works recognized by the Eastern Church. Revelation was not included universally among the authorized books of the New Testament for the first millennium of its existence.

Even then the dispute was not over. Another five hundred years passed and Martin Luther, while keeping Revelation in the Bible, said he wished he could throw the book into the Elbe River. His colleague in the sixteenth century Reformation, Ulrich Zwingli, showed no concern for Revelation, bluntly declaring it is "not a biblical book." John Calvin, Protestantism's first great systematic theologian and one seldom at a loss for words, protested with silence by writing commentaries on every book of the New Testament except Revelation.

Today the churches of the Orthodox tradition omit Revelation entirely from the scriptural texts assigned for reading during Sunday worship. The lectionaries of the Roman Catholic and mainline Protestant traditions rarely suggest passages from Revelation.

Paradoxically, no other Biblical book has influenced the hymnody of the church more profoundly:

Crown Him with Many Crowns, the Lamb upon the Throne
All Hail the Power of Jesus' Name! Let Angels Prostrate Fall
Blessing and Honor and Glory and Power
Holy, Holy, Holy, Lord God Almighty
Glorious Things of Thee Are Spoken, Zion, City of our God
Shall We Gather at the River
Blessed Assurance, Jesus is Mine…

While the preaching ministry of the church overlooks Revelation, its songs of praise are raised from the pews, living testimony to the power of Revelation's images to touch our hearts even as they perplex our heads.

Jerome, the fourth century Bible translator, puzzling over the ancient manuscripts in his Bethlehem study, scratched his head as he reached the last book of the Bible, quipping that Revelation has as many riddles as words!

Seven stars, seven lamp stands, seven letters to seven churches, seven signs, seven seals, seven trumpets, seven bowls, 1000 years, 144,000 souls,

666 – how are we to interpret such numbers? How are we to make sense of a bizarre beast rising from the sea with ten horns and seven heads, a creepy creature climbing out of the ground with two horns like a lamb and speaking like a dragon, and a scarlet monster bearing a great harlot drunk on blood? Who is that woman clothed with the sun, with the moon under her feet, and on her head a crown of twelve stars; and why is that enormous dragon intent on devouring her newborn child? What is the significance of the colors in Revelation: purple clothes; a golden sash; an emerald green rainbow; white, red, black, and pale green horses? To whom is the author referring in mentioning the Nicolaitans, Gog and Magog, and Apollyon the locust king? Many have tried reading Revelation but given up, assuming the book is a giant cryptogram for which they lack the key.

Words and images offensive to modern sensibilities constitute another excuse for relegating Revelation to the last biblical book some want to take seriously. Not much reading is required to encounter violent stories, sexist symbols, and references appearing anti-Semitic.

A trumpet blows, and there comes forth hail and fire, mixed with blood, scorching a third of the earth. A sickle swings, and blood flows as high as a horse's bridle for two hundred miles. A bowl of wrath is poured, and people gnaw their tongues in agony, cursing God for their pains and sores. Birds gorge themselves on human flesh in what the author of Revelation calls "God's great supper." Torment and torture, death and destruction, the violent images of warfare – why concern ourselves with these when the gospel teaches God is love?

Then there are the sexist metaphors. Rome is damned in Revelation for being a "great harlot…the mother of whores." The nameless prophet with whom Revelation's author takes so much exception is dismissed summarily as "that woman Jezebel who…is seducing my servants into fornication." The only two "positive" female images in the book belong to the bride of the Lamb and the woman clothed with the sun, both depicted as pure, passive, and powerless.

That the language of Revelation reflects the patriarchal world of the author's time is expected. Nevertheless, the exclusive depiction of women as virtuous or prostitutes, coupled with the dominate male image throughout of an almighty warrior king, fail to do justice to the first century women leaders of the church, Paul's teaching that "in Christ there is neither male nor female," or Jesus' radically inclusive example.

Then there is the author's apparent anti-Semitic attitude. With so few direct quotes, often overlooked is that there are more allusions to Hebrew scripture in Revelation than in any of the gospels, the book of Acts, or all of the epistles. Of the 404 verses comprising the book, 278 contain one or more references to the Jewish law, prophets, and writings. While evident that the author appreciates and respects the church's Jewish roots, his lambasting of "those who say that they are Jews and are not, but are a synagogue of Satan" is almost too strong to stomach at a time when understanding between the world's great religions is imperative for world peace.

Along with perplexing images and offensive language, a third rationalization for neglecting Revelation lies in the book's association with end-of-time cults, survivalist paranoia, and zealot evangelists. Though seldom expressed aloud, the thinking goes that if the last book in the Bible is favorite reading for those counting the days until the earth's demise, those forming society's fanatical fringe, and those intent on judging others as "saved" or "damned," then they can have it.

As a result others take the book and run with it, creating widely circulated popular works purportedly based upon Revelation. Hal Lindsey was the first to capitalize on the market in the 1970s when his "non-fiction" best-selling book, *The Late Great Planet Earth*, sold 40,000,000 copies. Today that number has been more than matched by the admittedly fictional *Left Behind* series. No longer reserved for the shelves of Christian bookstores, such books are found on the tables of your nearest bookstore chain or airport newsstand. Writes Tim LaHaye:

> The book of Revelation is easily the most fascinating book in the Bible, for it gives a detailed description of the future. Everyone is interested in what is going to happen to them and their loved ones after death, what will happen to the people of the earth, and what the future holds for this planet. Revelation not only answers all these questions but also gives them in great detail... In fact, if the incredible interest in our fiction series *Left Behind* (written with Jerry Jenkins), which has remained at the top of the best-seller list every month since it appeared four years ago, is any indication, the fascination for this subject is increasing.[4]

People are fascinated by the subjects he lists. People are longing for answers to the questions he raises. Unfortunately, contrary to LaHaye's reading, Revelation offers tantalizingly few details regarding the future. In company with the other biblical prophets, the author's eyes focus on issues of the present far more than they peer into the future. The words of this ancient prophet are not so much predictions of upcoming events as they are critical commentary on human behavior in light of God's will for the world.

---

[4] LaHaye, Tim. *Revelation Unveiled*. Grand Rapids: Zondervan, 1999. Page 9.

Therein lays a fourth explanation – perhaps the real reason – why Revelation is ignored, neglected, misunderstood, and disregarded. While we acknowledge Revelation's perplexing images, its offensive writing, and the preference not to be associated with those who embrace the work as if it were the only book in the Bible, what no one wants to admit is that Revelation's message hits too close to home for us to remain cozy, content, and comfortable.

"Is God in control of the universe or not?" Revelation answers with a resounding yes! But it also points out principalities and powers staking their claim on our government, judicial system, corporations, unions, medical establishment, financial institutions, and social gatherings.

"Is Christ truly the Lord of heaven and earth?" Revelation affirms Jesus as the only one worthy of our prayer and praise! But it also reveals the idolatry plaguing a very human church, the other gods capturing our hearts, the false deities we give allegiance that cannot save us.

"Is the Holy Spirit strong enough to override the forces of evil in our world?" Revelation envisions a promised "new heaven and a new earth" in which "mourning and crying and pain will be no more!" But it also confronts our corporate complicity with the powers of death and challenges us to change our evil ways.

The author of Revelation is John. Ah, but which John? John is such a common name.

Tradition holds that John the Apostle is the author of the gospel, the three letters, and Revelation. However, by the late 3rd or early 4th centuries the church historian, Eusebius, was postulating that the letters and Revelation had a different author than the gospel – someone he called "John the Presbyter." Now modern scholarship argues that the John who wrote the gospel (and possibly the first letter) is different than the John who wrote Revelation, with neither being the Beloved Disciple. The arguments are based on literary style, word choice, and grammatical constructs. Yet listening to the corpus of Johannine literature read aloud reveals enough theological similarity to suggest that if they were not written by the same person, at least the authors were thinking along similar lines.

So mystery remains regarding which John wrote Revelation. John the Apostle? John the Evangelist? John the Presbyter? John of Patmos? We shall be content simply to refer to the author of Revelation as "John," and we shall use the name "John" freely in this book in relation to the entire Johannine school of authors.

John prophesies from the island of Patmos in the Aegean Sea, a barren ribbon of rock seven-and-a-half miles long with no source of fresh water. He writes he is exiled for preaching God's word and witnessing to Christ Jesus. Peace activist Daniel Berrigan, confined to a "24-hour lockup, two in a cell hardly large enough for one, sharing space with mice, rats, flies and assorted uninvited fauna," poses an insightful question: "What kind of preaching brings that kind of punishment?"[5]

Is it not precisely the same kind of preaching which subjected the Hebrew prophets to persecution? Is it not exactly the same kind of preaching which led to the conspiring of religion and government to crucify Jesus? Is it not the same kind of preaching which caused Allan Boesak's imprisonment in Johannesburg, and Martin Luther King, Jr. being locked up in Birmingham? Isn't it fascinating these twentieth century spiritual leaders, having come up against the powers, found themselves not only incarcerated for their faith, but also drawn in their writing to the images of Revelation?[6]

What kind of preaching brings that kind of punishment? It is preaching to those who have power at their disposal which could be but is not being utilized to empower others, preaching to those who enjoy relative privilege compared to the poverty-stricken, preaching to those who have prospered materially but hunger spiritually. It is preaching that holds up a mirror allowing those who profit from participation in Western society to see themselves in light of God's revealed will for all humankind. It is preaching that asks: what spirit is upon us that we do so little to join Jesus in his ministry "to bring good news to the poor, to proclaim release to the captives and recovery of sight to the blind, to let the oppressed go free."

Harvard's Elisabeth Schüssler Fiorenza observes that Revelation inspires hope among those struggling for justice, serving as a source of strength for those living on society's margins. Perceived by the oppressed as a book naming the powers of evil, it offers a vision of justice and well-being motivating "the reader to engage in resistance and struggle for change."[7]

Revelation is a book we ignore at our peril. So warns Revelation's author in the last chapter, cautioning us not to add or detract from the words of his prophecy. But there also is a blessing promised in the first chapter to those who read aloud, hear, and keep what has been written in Revelation.

So set this study aside and open your Bible to the last book. Begin with Revelation 1:1 and read through Revelation 22:21. Read it in one setting. Read it aloud. If possible, read it with others without stopping for discussion. It will take an hour and a half.

Let the images trigger your imagination, the language stir up your emotions, and the rhetoric convict your heart and convince your soul to

---

[5] Berrigan, Daniel. *The Nightmare of God*. Portland: Sunburst Press, 1983. Pages 3-4.

[6] In addition to Berrigan's *The Nightmare of God*, see Boesak's *Comfort and Protest* as well as King's *Letter from a Birmingham Jail*.

[7] Fiorenza. Pages 10-11.

commit your life to engaging in the battle between God and the gods. Listen to what the Spirit is saying to the churches. Doing so will leave you no longer at ease.

Let anyone who has an ear listen
to what the Spirit is saying
to the churches.

2 "TO THE ANGEL OF THE CHURCH..."

An "Angel Tree" fills our living room at Christmas. With airy white gowns, gilded butterfly wings, and radiant golden halos, angel ornaments fly suspended from the boughs and lounge gracefully on the needles, the largest on top of the tree heralding the good news of Jesus' birth. Angel figurines hover over our entertainment unit, adorn our bookshelves, and gather on our coffee table – gifts accumulated from years serving the church. Some play stringed instruments. Others sound elongated trumpets. Most kneel in prayer. Then there are the chubby cherubs, somehow out of season with their mischievous grins.

Angels certainly have enjoyed a phenomenal rise in popularity over the last thirty years. Billy Graham published *Angels: God's Secret Agents* in 1975, when few books on the subject were on the market. Amazon.com now lists 250,000 "angel" titles. Google the word "angel" and 270,000,000 entries appear.

Medieval scholastics allegedly tried computing the number of angels that could dance on the point of a needle. I gave up counting our collection. The Risen Christ orders John to write to seven angels in the opening chapters of Revelation, each associated with a specific local church in the ancient Roman province of Asia. Numerous other angels are found throughout Revelation – one rather famous one named Michael – engaged in what feels like the most un-angelic of behaviors.

Like medieval painters, renaissance sculptors, and stained-glass artists, popular Western culture portrays angels as lovely spiritual beings, almost always feminine-looking, with kind faces and gentle demeanors, offering peace, hope, love, and joy. People today testify about guardian angels protecting them from harm and saving them from death. Assuming the essential purpose of an angel is to make them happy, individuals look for angels to bring answers to their prayers, and credit them with conveying blessings as mundane as parking spaces.

Such perceptions bear little resemblance to the angels of scripture. Yes, angels may take on human form, as in the story of Abraham and Sarah entertaining angels unaware. But in the few passages with physical descriptions of angels, these other-worldly creatures certainly do not resemble human beings with sprouted wings! Moreover, from the scriptural point-of-view, the primary function of angels is to deliver God's messages and to carry out God's orders. Biblically speaking, angels do not act as personal security guards, fulfill inconsequential whims, or answer to our beck and call. Angels exist to serve God.

While popular culture would domesticate God's angels, the seven angels standing before the throne of God in Revelation 8-9, for example, are anything but tame. One by one, on God's orders, they unleash the fiery hailstorms, erupting volcanoes, poisoning pollution, light-depriving eclipses, locust blights, and fatal plagues of God's wrath.

The language is apocalyptic. While rarely chosen as a writing style today, the first readers of Revelation were familiar with the genre. Apocalyptic literature is highly stylized in structure and tends to be quite similar in form. Typically the author is unknown. An heroic historical figure receives a secret vision from an angelic being, who may also interpret the vision. The heroic figure lives during a time of great evil in which God's people are experiencing persecution, suffering, and death. Revealed is a coming cosmic battle, involving numerous catastrophic events, at the end of which good prevails, God delivers judgment, and a new world is created. Mythical beasts, vivid imagery, poetic metaphors, and extensive symbolism are common, making literal interpretation inappropriate. In apocalyptic literature, authors write from a past point of view, referencing the future, using dramatic language to give prophetic words of promise and warning regarding what God's people are experiencing in the present.

Daniel and Revelation are the most extended pieces of apocalyptic literature in the Bible. Snippets exist elsewhere in scripture, among them Ezekiel 38-39 and "the little apocalypse" of Mark 13. There are numerous non-canonical examples as well – several composed from 200 to 100 BCE, and then another flourish in the second and third centuries CE.[8] Among the most famous pre-dating Revelation are the Sibylline Oracles, I Enoch, II Baruch, and IV Ezra.

Because authors tend to write in apocalyptic style during particularly oppressive times, the natural assumption has been that John wrote during a

---

[8] The contemporary convention of BCE for "Before the Christian Era" and CE for "Christian Era," rather than the traditional BC and AD, is used throughout this book.

period when Christians were undergoing severe persecution. However, with respect to the late first century when Revelation was written, modern scholarship can find no evidence supporting the conventional wisdom.

While Christians always were subject to the possibility of persecution for not worshipping the gods of the empire, and while there was a brutal outbreak of persecution in the city of Rome during Nero's reign, actual persecution in the late 1st century was localized and limited. Another century would pass before widespread persecution became the norm under Emperor Diocletian (303-311 CE).[9]

Yes, Domitian was an egomaniacal despot. Yes, Domitian issued orders for everyone to proclaim him "Lord," "God," and "Savior." Yes, during Domitian's reign there was an occasional martyrdom. But nothing discovered to date in any literary work contemporary with Revelation, and nothing unearthed in any archaeological dig with ruins from that period, suggests Domitian was crucifying Christians on crosses, feeding Christians to lions, or carrying out a genocidal pogrom in the Roman province of Asia. So, something else must be behind John's choice of genre.

Moreover, a close reading of Revelation 1 does not even require us to conclude that John was on Patmos because Domitian exiled him as punishment. John simply writes he is there "on account of the word of God and the testimony of Jesus." Because John wrote in an apocalyptic style, the long-standing assumption has been that John was incarcerated in a penal colony. Perhaps that is true; but John's own words may only mean he sailed to the island on a mission trip. So, if it was not to secret his message past the guards, why did John pick this known but unusual style of literature?

When John wrote Revelation, the Roman Empire was the only superpower. Under Roman rule, transportation, communication, and commerce were good. Safety was guaranteed by the Roman legions. The world was at peace, the *Pax Romana*, the "Peace of Rome." Historical evidence suggests that life was not all that bad for Christians in the late first century CE. To the contrary, in the safety and security provided by Rome, Christians would have prospered.

"Unfortunately, John has a problem," Brian Blunt, then Professor of New Testament at Princeton Theological Seminary, proclaimed at a baccalaureate service:

> The problem is this: very few of the people in his churches actually believe that there *is* a problem... As long as his

---

[9] Anderson, Paul. "Revelation 17:1-14" in *Revelation as a Critique of Empire, Interpretation: A Journal of Bible and Theology*. Volume 63. Number 1. January 2009. Page 61.

Christians didn't profess and then live out their Christianity in a way that made them stand out and act up for the kind of world that God desired rather than the kind of world Rome desired, everything was fine. Most of the people in his seven churches were doing so well, were so politically, socially, economically, and spiritually successful, were living such comfortably peaceful lives as a result of their careful, courteous, conforming, compliant, coddling, accommodating *Christian* conduct...[that] they had too much to lose. Even though John saw the world spinning completely out of control, even though he understood that the forces of darkness were set to prevail upon and destroy the forces of light, too much in the churches of Ephesus, Smyrna, Pergamum, Thyatira, Sardis, Philadelphia, and Laodicea was *relatively calm*. John saw a category five hurricane blowing down the walls of creation itself. John's church people were in their living rooms watching *Survivor* and *Roman Idol* and listening to spiritual CDs.[10]

Perhaps John dusted off the apocalyptic genre to shock the people in his churches into an alternative understanding of the status quo. Many try arguing that he chose this genre because its meaning would be lost on Romans guards; but that cannot be the case, because only the most obtuse of Romans could fail to recognize that John considered Rome the epitome of an evil empire. Far more likely is that John penned an apocalypse to grab his people's attention long enough for them to grasp the systemic evil they had come to accept as good, in the hope that they would be motivated to change their ways.

The word "apocalypse" simply means an "unveiling," a "disclosure," a "revelation." John opens his apocalypse with the words "The revelation of Jesus Christ..." Please note the word is singular. John's intent is not to reveal to his readers a series of unfolding catastrophic events marking the end of the world, but to show them the rightful place of the Risen Christ in God's realm, along with its implications for their behavior in the here and now. To a Christian church not living faithfully in the time of an empire, among all the numerous gods vying for devotion, John means to remind them of who is God and who is not.

So the first chapter in John's apocalypse directs his readers' attention to the one on whom John wants their eyes focused:

---

[10] Blout, Brian K. "Pick a Fight!" in *Princeton Seminary Bulletin* (Vol. XXVI, No. 2, New Series, 2005). Page 128.

> I saw one like the Son of Man, clothed with a long robe and with a golden sash across his chest. His head and his hair were white as white wool, white as snow; his eyes were like a flame of fire; his feet were like burnished bronze, refined as in a furnace; and his voice was like the sound of many waters. In his right hand he held seven stars, and from his mouth came a sharp, two-edged sword, and his face was like the sun shining with full force. (Revelation 1:13-16)

According to the gospel accounts, the title "Son of Man" is one Jesus used for himself. It also is found in Daniel 7:13-14, which reads:

> I saw one like a son of man coming with the clouds of heaven; and he came to the Ancient One and was presented before him. To him was given dominion and glory and kingship, that all peoples, nations and languages should serve him. His dominion is an everlasting dominion that shall not pass away, and his kingship is one that shall never be destroyed.

Clearly John sees the exalted Christ as the one who exercises ultimate authority over the universe, the one whose sovereignty is greater than the emperor's, and the one to whom the church needs to give its sole allegiance. This one, whom the angels laud in Revelation 5 with the very same praises they sing to God in Revelation 4, has something to say to the seven churches of Asia. Since in apocalyptic literature the number seven carries a symbolic connotation of completeness, Revelation is intended for the church in its entirety – for every church in every place at every time. Even the letters to the individual churches in Revelation 2-3 are meant for everyone. "Let anyone who has an ear listen to what the Spirit is saying to the churches," John admonishes seven times.

Why did John address his apocalypse to these specific seven churches? He had other options. We know, for example, there were churches in the Asian cities of Hierapolis and Colossae. And why do the individual letters to these seven churches appear in the particular order they do? Absent any explicit reason in the text, various theories arise.

One theory is that John picked them because of their geographic location and his wanting to send a secret visual picture affirming the Christian church as the continuing presence of God's light in the world, the church being the successor of the synagogue as the true Israel. Draw a curved line between Ephesus and Laodicea, so the theory goes, and then draw lines straight up from that line to the other five cities, and something akin to a menorah appears. It takes imagination to see the sign and gullibility to accept the theory. Such a flight of fantasy has no basis in the text. Moreover, a theology of supersessionism is contrary to God's covenant with the Jewish people continuing unabridged.

Another group of theories assumes each of the seven churches represents a particular period of history. The argument goes that the issues peculiar to each church parallel issues arising in each respective age. So, for example, Ephesus represents the New Testament church, Smyrna represents the church under persecution until the conversion of Constantine; and so forth. According to such schemes, one of the seven churches represents the time of the Reformation, another the Enlightenment. Laodicea always represents the last age before the end of the world.

Such theories are pure eisogesis – reading into the text what the theorist wants to find there, rather than reading out of the text what actually is there. Such theories require one to believe John wrote of periods about which he could know nothing, and that the first recipients of the Revelation had no understanding of that to which the letters refer. Moreover, the purveyors of such theories, no matter the century, inevitably believe they are living in the age of Laodicea (when everything is awful and there is absolutely nothing good to say about the state of the church) and they then redefine the previous time periods accordingly. Lacking is a basic understanding of the biblical meaning of prophecy. Prophets do not gaze into crystal balls to predict the future with specificity. Rather, in light of God's nature, prophets pronounce God's word on the present moment, with the future becoming a consequence of acceptance or rejection of God's will.

John's wisdom in selecting these seven churches will become evident in the following chapters as we discern key issues facing each in its context. The reason for the order in which the seven letters appear is obvious by looking at a map

Appendix A contains a topological map of western Anatolia. One archaeological axiom is that roads do not move, especially in mountainous regions. Roads are built where easiest, and then are repaired or replaced in the same location, civilization after civilization. Wherever possible roads go around mountains instead of over them. The road system in this part of western Turkey today runs along the coast and through the valleys, suggesting that in the ancient Roman province of Asia the letters traveled the natural postal route, from Ephesus to Smyrna to Pergamum to Thyatira to Sardis to Philadelphia to Laodicea.

John wrote Revelation as a single unit, to be read aloud in one sitting, within all seven churches. What John wrote to each of the seven churches was intended to be read and appropriated by all the others. The order in which the names of the seven churches appear is likely the same as the order in which John's apocalypse circulated.

Each letter follows the same seven-element format, though the sequencing of the sections sometimes varies. They all begin with identical greetings – "To the angel of the church in…" A description of the Risen Christ follows, typically but not exclusively taken from Revelation 1. Then comes a word of praise, beginning with the words "I know…," accompanied by a listing of what the church is doing right. A word of criticism is next, typically starting with "But I have this against you…" A warning is attached indicating what is in store if the church does not change its behavior, along with a promise of reward if it does. Finally there is the common exhortation: "Let anyone who has an ear…" There are a couple exceptions: neither Smyrna nor Philadelphia receives criticism, and Laodicea is denied praise.

Appendix B contains an analysis of each letter by section, and the following chapters examine each section in detail. You may wish to take time now to identify the various sections in each letter, before returning to the conclusion of this chapter and the question: To whom is John referring when he addresses each letter "To the angel…"?

Again, multiple fanciful theories abound. One theory is that the reference is to the seven angels surrounding God's throne; but this is unlikely since those seven angels are called upon to carry out God's will against the unfaithful, which include the angels of the seven churches being called into account.

Another theory – perhaps the earliest theory – would have us believe John is addressing the "guardian angels" of the churches; but this theory is problematic since the seven churches are not being protected from evil. Indeed, according to John, they are participating in it.

Still a third theory is that the word "angel" is a synonym for "bishop" – the religious leader of each church. One advocate of this theory even suggests that "that woman Jezebel, who calls herself a prophet" is the bishop of Thyatira's wife! But the word "bishop" is not a synonym for "angel," the linkage to the false prophet is pure conjecture, and the only one in Revelation who appears to have a bishop's oversight responsibility for the seven churches is John himself.

Walter Wink, Auburn Theological Seminary's Professor of Biblical Theology, is helpful in unraveling this mystery. He argues that the angel of each church "…is not something separate from the congregation, but must somehow represent it as a totality. Through the angel, the community seems to step forth as a single collective entity…" He writes:

> …the fact that the angel is actually addressed suggests that it is more than a mere personification of the church, but the actual

spirituality of the congregation as a single entity... As the corporate personality or felt sense of the whole, the angel of the church would have no separate existence apart from the people. But the converse would be equally true: the people would have no unity apart from the angel. Angel and people are the inner and outer aspects of one and the same reality. The people incarnate or embody the angelic spirit; the angel distills the invisible essence of their totality as a group... The one cannot exist without the other.[11]

Wink finds confirmation in the fact that in each letter the pronoun "you" is always singular. Reading the letters in English, it is easy to assume the "you" is plural, referring to the people within each congregation. But it is the angel of each church who is being addressed, the angel of each church whose works are known, the angel of each church who is given praise or blame, the angel of each church who is called to repentance, and the angel of each church who is offered a promise.

Angels are spirits commissioned to deliver messages from God and to carry out God's orders. From John's point of view, the angels of the churches are doing neither. They are not bearing a faithful witness to the God who is the absolute sovereign and ultimate judge of the world; and, in Wink's words, each is making "some other goal its idol."[12]

Actually, the angel of any church is easy to identify. Look for the angel in the statement a church makes about itself in its architecture, in its internal power structures, in the way it handles conflict, or in its spending priorities. Is the church hospitable to newcomers, or does one have to be a member for thirty years to be accepted? Is the church committed to ministries of justice and compassion, or is it spiritually naval-gazing? Does membership confer status in the community, or is it inclusive of those on the margins of society? Is the church dying as it remembers some glorious past, or is it living in expectation of what God has in store?[13]

"[Angels] are everywhere in the Book of Revelation..." writes Daniel Berrigan. "They stand at distance from creation, they speak from within, as we say, the soul of things... What is one to make of a religion that loses all

---

[11] Wink, Walker. *Unmasking the Powers: The Invisible Forces That Determine Human Existence.* Philadelphia: Fortress Press, 1986. Page 70.

[12] Wink. Page 78.

[13] Wink, Pages 73-78.

sense of spirit? ...Not seeing them? What this entails, I think, is…a loss of conscience, of right order, of the rigor and discipline of love."[14]

Marcus Borg and John Dominic Crossan add that "Whenever angels speak in the Bible, it is time to listen carefully."[15]

It also is time to pay attention when the Risen Christ speaks to the angels.

***Let anyone who has an ear listen
to what the Spirit is saying
to the churches.***

---

[14] Berrigan. Page 10.

[15] Borg, Marcus J. and John Dominic Crossan. *The First Christmas: What the Gospels Really Teach About Jesus's Birth.* New York: HarperOne, 2007. Page 189.

3 EPHESUS

Barges dredge the river running through this Midwestern city, keeping the channel open for ships hauling grain, ore, and oversized manufactured goods. Crisscrossing interstate highways transport distant-bound tourists and mall-bound shoppers. Loyalty runs deep to the locally-headquartered corporate giants which preserved the city's prosperity even during the Depression.

During the 1960s a suburb developed on the river bluff. Centrally placed on prime residential real estate is First Church, a mission start which never reached its potential.[16]

The problem is not location, timing, or demographics. Chartered as the metropolitan area began twenty years of sustained growth, increasing by more than one hundred thousand new residents, the congregation broke ground, built a first unit, and drew up architectural plans for future construction. But then a bitter fight over scriptural interpretation erupted.

One Sunday morning during an adult Bible study, the pastor's spouse shared her belief that Genesis 1 is not be taken literally, that the creation account is a faith story rather than a scientific fact, and that she had no problem seeing God's creative activity within the process of evolution.

Upon hearing, one church leader hurled her red-lettered Bible across the room at the pastor's spouse's chest!

---

[16] Throughout this book actual congregations are the basis for the illustrations, though their names have been changed.

²:¹*Write to the angel of the church in Ephesus! Thus saith the one holding the seven stars in his right hand, the one walking about amid the seven lamp stands of gold.*

²*I know your accomplishments, both the hard work and your patience, and that you cannot tolerate evil. And that you questioned the ones saying they themselves are apostles, only they are not. You found them to be false.*

³*You possess patience. You endured on account of my name. You have not tired.*

⁴*Nevertheless, I hold against you that you abandoned your first love.*

⁵*Remember, therefore, from what state you have fallen! Repent! Do the earlier works! Otherwise, if you should not repent, I will come to you and I will remove your lamp stand from its place.*

⁶*However, you have this: that you hate the deeds of the Nicolaitans that I myself hate.*

⁷*Whoever has an ear, hear what the spirit is saying to the churches! To the victor I will grant permission for him/her to eat from the tree of life that is in God's paradise.*

The Cayster River makes its way to the Aegean Sea, depositing fine silt and alluvial debris eroding from hillsides and mountains. The battle against nature to keep the river navigable lost centuries ago, today the spectacular ruins of Ephesus sit six miles inland. But at the time of Revelation's writing, the Supreme Metropolis of the province of Asia was a cosmopolitan commercial center connected to the coast, where east met west as travelers traversed the trade route to the riches of the orient.

Set aside Sunday school notions of a quaint, quiet, pastoral village. First century Ephesus was a bustling port with a booming economy, streets teeming with merchants from every corner of the known world. Population statistics are notoriously difficult to compute accurately, but an estimate of a quarter million people would not be far off. The great theater on the western slope of Mt. Panayir could seat twenty-five thousand. The stadium sat seventy thousand for the Pan-Ionian Games – the ancient rival of the Olympics.

Herodotes writes that Ephesus was founded when Androklos, son of the King of Athens, formed a Greek trading colony around 1000 BCE. Overlooked by the Greek historian is that people lived in Ephesus for hundreds of generations before the Athenians arrived.

Unearthed by the archeological digs of the Ephesus Museum are the sun-dried bricks, polished grindstones, bronze tools, game animal bones, mussel and oyster shells of a hunting and fishing settlement dating to 6000 BCE. Uncovered by relatively recent excavations are artifacts indicating Ephesus was the capital city of the Ahiyava Kingdom around 3000 BCE. A tomb discovered during demolition for a parking lot reveals the Mycenaeans lived in the city around 1400 BCE. Meeting the Athenians on the shore were the Karians. Subsequently the Lydians, Persians, Macedonians, Ptolemies, and Seleucids all governed Ephesus. It finally came under Roman rule in 133 BCE. Clearly the residents of first century Ephesus were multicultural by ancestry.

According to tradition John and Mary the mother of Jesus made their homes in Ephesus. One can drive up a mountainside and take a pleasant forested walk to the traditional site of Mary's house, or pause in the ruins of St. John's Church before the four marble columns and the gravestone marking the traditional site of the apostle's tomb. However, be advised that "the traditional site" usually means evidence supporting the claim is sparse.

By contrast, substantial scriptural documentation exists for Paul residing in Ephesus, headquartering a significant portion of his missionary efforts there.

According to Acts, Paul sailed into Ephesus on his way from Corinth to Syria, accompanied by Priscilla and Aquila who remained in the city, no doubt as seeds for a new church start. After traveling through Galatia (modern Ankara) where the locals questioned his apostleship, Paul fulfilled a promise to return to Ephesus, living there for two years, the first three months preaching in the synagogue, then teaching in a lecture hall. During this stay Paul sent his first letter to the Corinthians, writing eloquently, profoundly, and memorably to that deeply conflicted mission church about the nature, power, and greatness of love.

While in Ephesus, Paul baptized with the Holy Spirit those who knew only John the Baptist's baptism for repentance. He also performed healings so extraordinary that, according to the scriptures, simply being touched by Paul's handkerchief was enough to drive out evil spirits. Recognizing God's power at work in Paul, the city's magicians publicly burned the Ephesian scrolls containing the formulas for their spells, valued at 50,000 silver coins – the equivalent in typical daily wages of 137 years of work. Most notably, Paul caused a riot in Ephesus by confronting the vested interests of local businesses tied to the Temple of Artemis – particularly the livelihood of Demetrius, the silversmith who fashioned shrines of the goddess for pilgrims.

"Great is Artemis of the Ephesians!" yelled the mob as it took to the streets, making its way to the great theater. "Great is Artemis of the Ephesians!" the riotous crowd chanted in unison, over and over, again and again and again, anger rising with every repetition. For two terrifying hours the horde held two of Paul's companions captive, the cry "Great is Artemis of the Ephesians!" vibrating across the city.

In the panoply of gods, Artemis was greatest in Asia. Her Ephesian temple was one of "The Seven Wonders of the Ancient World." Actually Artemis is the name of the Greek goddess the Athenian immigrants associated with the native goddess, Kubaba. Later the Romans associated her with their goddess Diana.

A six-inch terracotta statue of Kubaba dating to 5750 BCE, on display at the Museum of Anatolian Civilization in Ankara, depicts her as a big breasted, huge hipped, obscenely obese goddess of nature, arms perched on female lions, squatting to give birth to Attis, the god of vegetation. By John's time this goddess had slimmed down considerably. The statue of Artemis in the Ephesus Museum embodies a tall lovely figure wearing a long skirt decorated with rows of deer, goats, bulls, griffins, and bees. An alternating pattern of rosettes and bees adorns her belt, while necklaces of grapes, pearls, and precious stones grace her neck and chest. The animal motif appears as well on the first two layers of her three-tiered crown, topped with a representation of her temple.

Considerable debate surrounds the many protrusions from her abdomen. Some believe the goddess has grown repulsively grotesque multiple breasts. Others conclude she sports the testicles of a herd of bulls. While the ancients considered Artemis the mother goddess of Anatolia, little other than vivid imagination supports the theory that she was a lascivious fertility goddess around whom no male was safe, her priestesses no more than cultic prostitutes.

Artemis also was known as the goddess who watched over women during childbirth, the goddess of the animals of the forest, and the goddess of the painless hunt. Perhaps best is to think of her simply as the queen bee. Of all the creatures on her dress, bees are prominent. Her priestesses were called *melissae* or worker bees, and her priests *megabyzi* or drones. Even the coins minted in Ephesus featured the bee symbol of their goddess. For the Ephesians, whose prosperous city buzzed with life, Artemis reigned at the center of their hive.

Little remains of the Temple of Artemis save a single column in the middle of a marsh. But the Roman author Pliny the Younger describes the first-century temple as four hundred thirty feet long, two hundred sixty feet wide, with one hundred twenty-seven columns each seventy feet tall. On display in London's British Museum is one of the thirty-six intricately carved column bases. Constructed of marble with a tiled wooden roof, the temple housed works of art, golden pillars, silver figurines, and four bronze statues of the Amazons – some on view at the New Hofburg Museum in Vienna.

The Temple of Artemis during John's time was the fifth erected to the goddess in Ephesus on the same site. The fourth temple – built around 550 BCE, designed by the famed Greek architect Chersiphron, and sponsored by the fabulously wealthy King Croesus of Lydia – won the spot on the list of ancient wonders. A madman named Herostratus, seeking immortality, torched it the same night Alexander the Great was born (July 21, 356 BCE), causing the Roman historian Plutarch to remark that Artemis must have been too busy taking care of the birth of Alexander to send help to her threatened temple.

The Ephesians rebuilt the temple in all its glorious wonder, using the same dimensions as the fourth temple, only on a built-up base. In 333 BCE Alexander offered to pay for the restoration, provided the Ephesians chiseled his name on the building. The city leaders refused his generosity, demurring diplomatically that it would not be fitting for one god to build a temple for another god. Alexander did not press the matter, leaving the city's pride intact.

"Great is Artemis of the Ephesians!" shouted Demetrius the silversmith. "Great is Artemis of the Ephesians!" roared the unruly rabble. None of the city's other gods rivaled Artemis. World traveling pilgrims flocked to her magnificent temple. To be within a bow's shot of her sanctuary guaranteed safety from enemies. To purchase one of her charms (called "Ephesian Letters") brought success. To call upon her as a witness ensured oaths were kept, testimonies were true, and contracts were binding.

Yet Paul's proclamation of the gospel in Ephesus posed such a threat that it started a riot. Who is God? Is it Christ? Is it Artemis? Demetrius knew in the battle of God versus the goddess, if Artemis did not win, life would end as he knew, enjoyed, and prospered in it. People following "The Way" (as Christianity first was called) do not purchase silver shrines. People who follow the Risen Christ do not bow before the goddess of economic prosperity, vested interests, and the marketplace.

Nor do they bow before the emperor.

Facing the great theater at the end of Harbor Street where the riot took place, if one turns right and walks along the Marble Way through the shopping agora to the picturesque second century Library of Celsus, and then left on Curetes Street and up the hill, beyond the palatial Slope Houses and though the Gate of Hercules lie the state agora and Domitian Square, home of the imperial cult.

Tourists photograph the Fountain of Trajan without noticing beneath the sculpture's foot that more than a millennium before Columbus these ancient Asians thought the earth was round. Another Kodak moment is found at the Temple of Hadrian with its intricately carved Corinthian columns, reconstructed friezes, and head of Tyche (the goddess of good luck). Neither edifice existed at the time of Revelation's writing.

Built during the first century and hidden behind the ruins of the Odeion (the small theater used for city council meetings) are the Temples to Roma and to the Divine Julius Caesar. Also erected during John's lifetime and particularly odious to Revelation's author – the ruins located on the opposite side of the street, rarely pointed out by tour guides, and seldom subject to picture taking by tourists – is the Temple to Domitian.

Julius Caesar (49 to 44 BCE) was the first emperor "deified" by the Roman Senate. Bestowed upon his adopted son Augustus (31 BCE to 14 CE), in recognition of and with gratitude for his ending the civil wars following Julius' assassination, were the titles *Dominus* ("Lord"), *Deus* ("God"), *Filius Deus* ("Son of God"), and *Sotar* ("Savior"). Those who prospered from the protection of the trade routes, safety guaranteed by the Roman legions, experienced the *Pax Romana* – a period of "peace" lasting some two centuries – as *euanggelion* ("good news"). One 9 BCE Asian inscription extols:

> The *most divine Caesar*...we should consider equal to *the Beginning of all things*.... Whereas the Providence which has regulated our whole existence...has brought our life to the climax of perfection in giving to us the emperor Augustus...who, being sent to us *as a Savior*, has put *an end to war*.... The birthday of *the god Augustus* has been for the whole world the beginning of *good news*.[17]

While no temples were built to Augustus in Rome, cities throughout the occupied territories competed for the privilege and prestige of constructing them. A city designated a center for the imperial cult was called a *neokoros* ("temple warden"). Technically, Roman citizens were to worship the emperor, with everyone else worshipping Rome personified in the goddess Roma.[18] Functionally emperor worship, worship of Roma, civic parades, public meals, lavish games, and imperial games were intertwined and served

---

[17] Italics added. Excerpted from Horsley, Richard. *The Liberation of Christmas*. New York: Crossroad, 1989. Page 27. Quoted in Borg, Marcus. J. *Reading the Bible Again for the First Time*. San Francisco: HarperCollins, 2001. Page 280.

[18] Worth. *The Seven Cities of the Apocalypse and Roman Culture*. New York: Paulist Press, 1999. Page 113.

to unify the provinces under Roman control by legitimizing its political authority as nothing less than the will of the gods.

During the nearly seventy years following the reign of Augustus, none of his successors emphasized emperor worship – not even Nero. Claudius went so far as to forbid worship of the emperor. No emperor demanded it until the reign of Domitian – the emperor who declared himself *Dominus et Deus* ("Lord and God"), requiring his subjects, including his wife, to address him by that title.

Ephesus received its first of four neokoroships during Domitian's reign. In the community John called home, he watched the Temple of Domitian being built on the city's highest point. A colossal sculpture of Domitian, perched to be seen from the sea's horizon, stood four times larger than any mere mortal, several sizes bigger than any statue to any other god, marble arm raised twenty-four feet above the ground, biceps bulging, fist closing. Lest anyone doubt or forget, sculpted on the giant altar to Domitian were instruments of the emperor's military might: swords, shields, quivers, armor, and helmets.

Of course, this powerful Roman government personified in Domitian was supported by taxation. Under a previous emperor, Vespasian, a fixed-sum per-person tax had been imposed on all the citizens of the province of Asia. With the crushing of the Jewish revolt and the destruction of the Jerusalem Temple in 70 CE, Vespasian added to that tax the amount that the Jewish population in the province had been sending to Palestine. Additionally, while the Temple dues had been limited to free adults males between the ages of twenty and fifty, Vespasian extended the tax to include all Jewish women, children, and slaves. In effect, at the time of John's writing, the Jewish population was being double-taxed.[19]

When Domitian then decreed that every resident of the empire, upon paying the hated Roman double-taxes, also had to proclaim "Caesar is Lord," pour a libation, and offer a pinch of incense to his idol, as far as John was concerned the gauntlet was thrown and war declared. How could Christians utter such an obscene confession? The church's creed is "Jesus is Lord."

Contrary to popular perception, Domitian's dictate did not trigger extensive persecution. Perhaps Roman officials were reluctant to enforce the death penalty because they recognized the emperor's egomaniacal madness. In time the Roman Senate would damn Domitian's memory (*Damnatio memoriae*), destroying his statues. Perhaps the Roman officials were unclear if Christianity was a Jewish sect or a separate religion. Exemptions written into law protected practitioners of the Jewish faith, so that they were permitted to

---

[19] Worth. …*Roman Culture*. Page 78.

pray *for* the emperor rather than *to* the emperor. Perhaps Roman officials in the distant provinces saw no need to stir up needless trouble.

Whatever the reason, modern scholarship has found no evidence of any widespread harassment, mistreatment, or discrimination against Christians during Domitian's reign. Roman officials paid little notice to Christians. Rather than initiating action against the faithful for refusing to say "Caesar is Lord," the evidence suggests the Romans singled out Christians occasionally for persecution, and then only in response to complaints received.

Shortly after Revelation's writing, in 112 CE, Emperor Trajan sent Pliny to the provinces north and east of Asia, advising him that:

> Christians should not be sought out. But if they are accused and handed over, they are to be punished, but only if they do not deny being Christians and demonstrate it by the appropriate act, i.e., the worship of our gods. Even if one is suspect because of past conduct, he or she is to be acquitted in view of repentance.[20]

While Pliny brought accused Christians to trial, he also admonished the people to stop the accusations. Perhaps typical thinking for other Roman officials, Pliny considered Christianity "a degenerate sort of cult carried to extravagant length" which would die out eventually.[21]

Nevertheless John considered Domitian's decree the ultimate fighting words. In the cosmic war between good and evil, the front had come to Ephesus…and to Smyrna…and to Pergamum…and to Thyatira…and to Laodicea…and to every other host city for the imperial cult. In John's mind the central threat posed by the Romans was not government persecution but an imperial government claiming God's rightful place in the people's lives.

Who is God? Is it Christ? Is it Caesar? In the battle between God and the gods, John believed it was time to take sides.

Following the greeting John lets the Ephesians know, in no uncertain terms, that the word he is about to pronounce comes from the Risen Christ. "These are the words of him who holds the seven stars in his right hand, who walks among the seven golden lamp stands." The verse contains no mystery. The titles are from the portrait John paints in chapter one: "… in the midst of the lamp stands I saw one like the Son of Man… In his right hand he held

---

[20] Anderson. Page 61.

[21] Thompson, Leonard L. *Revelation*. Nashville: Abingdon Press, 1998. Page 28.

seven stars…" In the last verse of the first chapter John explains "…the seven stars are the angels of the seven churches, and the seven lamp stands are the seven churches."

The number "seven" symbolizes completeness. As seven days constitute an entire week, "seven churches" refers to all the churches of the world in every place and at every time. "Lamp stands" better translates the Greek than the King James' "candlesticks," since candles were not yet invented. The New King James Version makes the correction.

Modern translations miss two important subtleties in the Greek of the first verse.

In connection with a description of the Risen Christ, the phrase *tade legei* is translated much too tamely by "These are the words of…" or "…is saying this." Hearing those two Greek words, the Ephesians immediately knew what followed would be a commanding word, a word of truth they could not ignore, a word directly from God. In the Septuagint (the Greek translation of the Hebrew scripture), *tade legei* is used whenever a prophet of God renders an oracle. *Tade legei* would have trumpeted in their ears like "*Thus saith the Lord*" rings in ours.

The phrase appears in the letters to the other six churches as well. Hearing seven times in succession "*Thus saith the Lord… Thus saith the Lord… Thus saith the Lord… Thus saith the Lord… Thus saith the Lord… Thus saith the Lord… Thus saith the Lord…*" underscores dramatically and unmistakably the source and authority of John's message.

Moreover, the Greek word in the first verse typically translated "holding" (*kratein*) is in the accusative rather than the usual genitive case. The distinction is the difference between clutching a piece of something and cupping an object in its entirety. John's point is clear: Domitian may believe his fist exercises dominion over the earth, but the truth is the Risen Christ holds the whole world in his hands.

Furthermore, while Domitian lives in far off Rome, incapable of knowing what is happening in every corner of his realm, the Risen Christ is "walking about" among the churches, seeing exactly what they are facing and what they are doing about it. "I know your works, your toil and your patient endurance. I know that you cannot tolerate evildoers." The Greek word for "toil" (*kopos*) connotes back-breaking labor, exhausting work, exertion causing sweat. Patience (*hupomone*) should not be understood as passive acceptance but as unbending determination. The Risen Christ knows the church in Ephesus is busy as bees in its resistance to evil.

In particular the Risen Christ knows the church has "tested those who claim to be apostles but are not, and found them to be false."

The generic definition of "apostle" is "one who is sent." In the ancient secular world apostles were ambassadors, envoys, representatives bearing messages. In early Christianity the word described messengers sent by God or

Christ. Some scriptures reserve the word for the first twelve disciples. Other passages use it to describe anyone who accompanied the twelve from John's baptism through Christ's ascension. In still other texts the word applies to everyone who witnessed the resurrection. Then there are verses in which the word pertains to missionaries. In Revelation, "apostle" is best understood with Second Peter as one sent to transmit to the churches the message of the prophets and of Jesus.

After the riot Paul moves on to Macedonia and Greece. Upon completing his third missionary journey, he returns to Jerusalem, stopping at several Aegean islands but bypassing Ephesus. Upon docking at Miletus, Paul summons the Ephesian elders and cautions them to test traveling teachers and congregational members who enter their flock like "*savage wolves*," claiming to speak for God but distorting the truth – false prophets intent on enticing the faithful to follow their message instead of Paul's.

Evidently the Ephesians took Paul's warning seriously, developing a reputation for heresy hunting. Ignatius compliments their vigilance in a letter written in 115 CE:

> I ought to be trained for the contest by you... [for] no heresy has a home among you. No, you do not so much as listen to anyone who speaks of ought else save concerning Jesus Christ in truth.... I have learned that certain persons passed through you from Syria bringing evil doctrine, whom you suffered not to sow seed in you, for you stopped your ears...[22]

While the Christians of Ephesus are praised for examining would-be apostles, the Risen Christ is not satisfied. Consistent with the oracles of the Hebrew prophets, the church is indicted in the courtroom of God's judgment: "But I have this against you, that you have abandoned the love you had at first."

Given their tireless efforts to be faithful to the gospel, to the teachings they learned from Paul at the lecture hall, to the truth of the apostles' message, the charge that they have "abandoned" (the Greek means "to forsake completely") the love they had at the first must have shocked them. On what grounds could a case be brought against them?

---

[22] English updated. Excerpted from *Ignatius to the Ephesians*, 3, 6, 9. Quoted in Ramsay, William . M. *The Letters to the Seven Churches*. Grand Rapids: Baker Book House, 1985. Page 241. Reprinted from the 1904 edition published by Hodder and Stoughton, London.

John may have perceived that hardness of heart which accompanies a dogged desire for doctrinal purity, something akin to the pharisaical self-righteousness with which Jesus took exception, what today we experience in the dogmatic judgments of religious fundamentalists. For John and his community, love is the essential nature of God and the indispensable characteristic of the Christian life.

In the First Letter of John (an extended sermon on love), the fourth chapter begins with John urging Christians to "test the spirits to see whether they are from God." But the context of that instruction is loving God and loving neighbor. Immediately preceding is this admonition: "Little children, let us love, not in word or speech, but in truth and action… This is his commandment: that we should believe in the name of his son Jesus Christ and love one another." Immediately following is this oft quoted passage: "Beloved, let us love one another, because love is from God; everyone who loves is born of God and knows God. Whoever does not love does not know God, for God is love…"

What Christian cannot quote from memory John 3:16? "For God so loved the world that he gave his only son, so that everyone who believes in him may not perish but may have eternal life."

Even the book of Revelation, for all its cycles of punishment, begins with the Risen Christ gently, reassuringly, lovingly bending down to place his hand on John's face, saying "Be not afraid." It ends with God bringing healing to the nations, personally wiping every tear from every eye.

Commenting on the relationship between love and forgiveness, which he considered "the whole genius of prophetic religion," the twentieth century ethicist Reinhold Niebuhr taught that the religiously hard of heart refuse to forgive others because they believe they themselves have little to be forgiven:

There is no deeper pathos in the spiritual life of [human beings] than the cruelty of righteous people. If any one idea dominates the teachings of Jesus, it is His opposition to the self-righteousness of the righteous… The criticism which Jesus leveled at good people had both a religious and a moral connotation. They were proud in the sight of God and they were merciless and unforgiving to [others]… Forgiving love is a possibility only for those who know that they are not good, who feel themselves in need of divine mercy, who live in a dimension deeper and higher than that of moral idealism.[23]

---

[23] Niebuhr, Reinhold. *Interpretation of Christian Ethics.* New York: Harper & Brothers, 1935. Chapter 7.

Could it be that in their zealousness to believe only what is right, the Ephesians forgot the right way to live? Could it be that in their eagerness to discern truth from falsehood, right from wrong, morality from immorality, the Ephesians forgot the last words in Jesus' greatest sermon: "Be merciful, even as God is merciful"? John believed "we love because God first loved us." Could it be that the Ephesians – in their testing, examining, questioning – no longer embraced others with love because they had forgotten the love they first received from God?

Or is the reference to forsaking completely their first love an indictment against a church focused on right interpretation of God's message but forgetful of that message's implications for the public square?

How concerned were the Christians in Ephesus with the Temple of Artemis? Were they still banking there, still making interest off loans extended in Artemis' name, still sealing contracts by an oath to Artemis, still profiting off tourists traveling to bow down before the statue within those temple walls?

How offended were the Christians in Ephesus by the imperial cult? Were they burning a pinch of incense at the altar to Domitian, paying their taxes to the Roman government, rationalizing it is alright given the benefits – increased security, greater prosperity, improved communication, expanded transportation – afforded by life in the Roman Empire? Did they pause before attending sporting events in the stadium dedicated to Emperor Nero, or worry about the values taught their children at the gymnasium, or enjoy leisurely days off at the baths?

The symbol of Roman power is the eagle. Did the Ephesians recognize the clash between that eagle and the cross any more than we distinguish the conflict between the cross and the flag? Or had life in the Roman Empire become so good in their great city that it was as easy for them as it is for us to overlook inconsistencies between the demands of faith and the desires of nation?

We citizens of the United States tend either to silence the prophetic word of God by compartmentalizing our lives into sacred and secular, or else to co-mingle church and state until we no longer distinguish the will of God from the actions of government. Quick to question the faith of others, had the Ephesians succumb to cooperating with the powers that be in the world? Have we?

The first of the Ten Commandments is: "You shall have no other gods before me." Jesus says the greatest commandment is: "You shall love the Lord your God with all your heart, and with all your soul, and with all your strength, and with all your mind." John's last word in his sermon on love is: "Little children, keep yourselves from idols." Martin Luther held that whatever we give our heart to is our god. Are we as Americans as prone as the Ephesians to abandoning our first love – the God revealed in Jesus Christ

– by compromising with the goddess of our marketplace and the god of our nation?

"Remember!" the Risen Christ instructs them. The verb is in the present imperative and best translated: "Remember and keep on remembering!" or "Remember and never forget!" Remember what? "Remember then from what you have fallen!" Remember and keep on remembering the love of God. Remember and never forget that acting on the basis of love toward God and neighbor has priority.

"Repent!" the Risen Christ demands. The verb is in the aorist imperative, indicating a distinct point in time. Turn around now. Change direction today. Make a definite and immediate decision to take a different course of action.

"Do!' the Risen Christ commands. Another imperative case verb. "Do the works you did at first!" The Ephesians knew how to love; but as time passed they took another way. They worked hard, accomplished much, and enjoyed a reputation for not tolerating evil. But patience, endurance, and tireless efforts are not enough. We almost can hear echoes of Paul's words to the Corinthians, penned while in Ephesus: "If I have all faith so as to remove mountains, but do not have love, I am nothing."

"If not," the Risen Christ continues, "I will come to you and I will remove your lamp stand from its place, unless you repent." Recalling that a "lamp stand" is Revelation's symbol for a local church, the warning returns us to the letter's first verse depicting the Risen Christ holding all the churches of the world in his hands. Surely if the Risen Christ has power enough to hold all the churches of the world in his hands, he also holds the authority to pluck the Ephesian congregation out of the Christian family and throw it away.

The image is almost too much to bear. John declares that even as the Ephesians examined the false prophets and rejected them for teaching the wrong message, so the Risen Christ will expel for eternity any church which – whatever its accomplishments – is examined and found less than loving.

Nevertheless hope remains. "Yet this is to your credit: you hate the works of the Nicolaitans, which I also hate." Please note that hated is the conduct of the Nicolaitans, not the Nicolaitans themselves, suggesting the Ephesians were able to distinguish between deeds and doers, sin and sinners, actions and persons. As long they could distinguish between the two, the possibility remained for them to love the one and hate the other, even as God does.

While no one knows precisely who the Nicolaitans are, their name's etymology is important. "Nicolaitans" is made up of two Greek words: *nike* meaning "to conquer" plus *laos* meaning "people." The Nicolaitans, then, are those who conquer the people. As we will discover in the letter to Pergamum, they conquer by seducing God's people into worshiping other gods.

Also remaining is a promise. The letter from the Risen Christ to the Ephesians concludes: "To everyone who conquers, I will give permission to eat from the tree of life that is in the paradise of God." The people of the known world believed Artemis reigned victoriously over the hearts of the Ephesians. In Rome, Domitian believed he reigned victoriously over his empire. But the word "conquer" in this promise is a play on the Nicolaitan reference. The Risen Christ calls upon the Ephesians to conquer – rather than to be conquered by – the temptation to follow anyone or anything other than the God of love. If they do, the God who removed Adam and Eve from the Garden of Eden for following a false message promises to reverse the same judgment now waiting the Ephesians.

Let anyone who has an ear listen
to what the Spirit is saying
to the churches.

4 SMYRNA

Except at Second Church, there is money in this town. Not old money. Not inherited money. Rather money for corporations from government contracts and tax abatements, as well as money for non-profits from federal earmarks and foundation grants.

A park and an elementary school are in every neighborhood. The business district thrives along downtown streets lined with herringbone patterned brick sidewalks, bannered lampposts, and rows of rosy red, snowy white, and more-bluish-than-purple petunias. Green spaces occupy areas once housing the poor.

In a politically conservative, upwardly mobile, get-out-the-vote kind of town, politicians laud the city's schools, libraries, and monuments. The Chamber of Commerce proudly points to amenities, selling the city as a good, clean, safe place to live, work, and raise a family. Religious leaders recognize their expected role as purveyors of traditional God and country values.

But the day came when the country went to war and the city's National Guard unit was called up. Naturally the residents support the troops who are, after all, their own children being sent to the front. Patriotic displays appear in store windows. People line parade routes to cheer marching soldiers. Sunday liturgies include nationalistic hymns. Anyone daring to question the President's motives for entering the war either is hassled to keep quiet or ostracized outright.

Fearing the threat of parishioners walking out, withholding funds, or firing pastors, no pulpit proclaims a single prophetic word, except at Second Church. That congregation knows all about social pressure, explosive pressure, silencing pressure. Threats took physical form earlier in its history when Second Church dared to raise questions about the hiring practices of the town's major employer. Members awoke to crosses burning on their lawns, torched by townspeople who never acknowledged their racism.

The preacher at Second Church has been criticizing the war in letters to the editor. The newspaper is publishing a story. Attached will be a photo of the American flag being removed from the sanctuary.

2:8 Write to the angel of the church in Smyrna! Thus saith the first and the last, who was dead but came back to life.

9 I know the crushing pressure you're under, and the extreme poverty (though you are rich), and the verbal abuse from those asserting themselves to be Jews (though they are not, but rather a synagogue of the adversary).

10 Fear nothing for yourself, what you are going to endure! Listen! The slanderer is going to put some of you into prison, so that you may be tested. You will have suffering for ten days. Be faithful unto death. I will give you the prize of life!

11 Whoever has an ear, hear what the spirit is saying to the churches! The victor will not be injured by the second death.

How strange to name a city after a smell. Especially this fragrance. "Smyrna" was the name of a perfume – like Chanel No. 5, Obsession, or Taboo – a scent released when a resin tapped from certain trees was dried, ground into powder, and placed in a sachet suspended around a person's neck, or was emulsified in oil for anointing. Its bouquet filled ancient sanctuaries – incense burned to the gods. The rich and famous sprinkled this aromatic substance as fabric freshener. Merchants stirred it into soothing cosmetic creams. Physicians mixed it with wine as a painkiller.

Yet the city of Smyrna never manufactured this perfume. No historian records this city smelled better than any other city in the ancient Roman province of Asia. Given the sanitary systems of the first century, on some stinking hot days the citizens surely wished it did!

To call the city "*Smyrna*" sounds stranger still when we realize the name was a synonym for "myrrh" – the third gift brought to the Christ Child by those mysterious magi from the east, symbolically foreshadowing his death on the cross. Nicodemus and Joseph of Arimathea, John tells us in the gospel, used a hundred Roman pounds of myrrh mixed with aloes to embalm Jesus' body and line his linen shroud – an enormous, extravagant, extremely expensive amount equivalent to approximately seventy-five pounds.

Myrrh, then, was the odor associated with the passage from life into death. However, Smyrna was not famous for building caskets. It enjoyed no reputation for having a school of mortuary science. Unlike Sardis, no burial mounds surrounded its city limits.

Scholars tell us the city did not take its name from the scent, but rather from Myrrha, the mother of Adonis. Always depicted as young and handsome, Adonis was the life-death-rebirth god of vegetation.

According to one version of the ancient myth, Myrrha lusts after her father, Theias. Horrified by her thoughts and feelings, she tries hanging herself, but is saved by a nursemaid who, believing incest less a sin than suicide, aids Myrrha's forays into her drunken dad's darkened bedroom. One night Theias lights a lamp, discovers what his daughter has been doing, and casts her out. A pregnant Myrrha flees, wandering the earth for nine months, until finally she prays she be allowed neither to live nor to die since what she has done is an abomination both to the living and to the dead. In answer, the gods turn her into a myrrh tree which, when its bark is struck and split by Theias' sword, gives birth to their son, Adonis. The Naiads care for the child, bathing him in droplets of myrrh – his mother's tears.

Whether named after the tragic Myrrha of Greek mythology or the fragrant resin of the myrrh tree, the ancients tied the city's name to the realities of death. Homer, a native, makes that connection in the *Illiad*. So does Plutarch in *Lives*. So does a legend originating in the surrounding region. According to the late Colin Hemer, Research Fellow at Tyndale House in Cambridge:

> The local story of Niobe became a universal type of mourning… Her father was Tantalus, already in Homer a type of the sinner suffering eternal torment. Her sister-in-law was Aëdon, transformed into a nightingale to lament her son. Her brother was Pelops, who was restored to life after being served up at a feast of the gods… The strength of local tradition in the district is notable…and perpetuated the picture of a city of suffering, a concept symbolized by its very name.[24]

---

[24] Hemer, Colin J. *The Letters to the Seven Churches of Asia in Their Local Setting.* Grand Rapids: William B. Eerdmans Publishing Company, 1989. Pages 58-59.

The Risen Christ instructs John to write to the angel of the church in Smyrna the "words of the first and the last, who was dead and came to life." The titles parallel verses in the first chapter of Revelation in which John reports hearing the Risen Christ say: "I am the first and the last and the living one. I was dead, and see, I am alive forever and ever."

To perceive the Risen Christ as "the first and the last" is to equate him with no one less than God. This particular title recalls the pronouncement of Isaiah 44:6-8, in which that prophet makes the same point John emphasizes throughout Revelation regarding who is God and who is not:

> Thus says the Lord, the King of Israel,
>   and his Redeemer, the Lord of hosts:
> I am the first and I am the last;
>   beside me there is no god.
> Who is like me? Let them proclaim it,
>   let them declare and set it forth before me.
> Who has announced from of old the things to come?
>   Let them tell us what is yet to be.
> Do not fear,
>   or be afraid;
> Have I not told you from of old and declared it?
>   You are my witnesses!
> Is there any god besides me?
>   There is no other rock;
>   I know not one.

If "the first and the last" is God, and if the Risen Christ is "the first and the last," then the emperor is not God, no matter how loudly Domitian claims the title. Nor is any military, economic, political, or religious leader, no matter how often those in power act as if they are. John insists Christians do not owe allegiance to any authority, loyalty to any leader, or devotion to any ideology. Such allegiance belongs only to the God revealed in the Risen Christ who calls us not to live in fear, acquiescing to the desires of the world's powerful, but rather with faith, witnessing to an alternative reality, a different set of priorities, life as God wills it for all on earth.

In the second half of this title for the Risen Christ, "came to life" better renders the Greek than "is alive" found in several translations. The verb is aorist rather than present, punctuating a specific moment in time, namely the instant of Christ's resurrection. The Smyrnians heard this movement from death to life as paralleling their city's history.

Located on the Aegean Sea thirty-five miles north of Ephesus, Smyrna was a Greek trading colony founded nearly a thousand years before Christ's birth. Situated on the coastal road, with a natural enclosed harbor, it quickly grew into a prosperous city. In time it dared to defy Sardis, the powerful neighboring capital city of the Lydian empire.

Consequently, near the end of the seventh century BCE, King Alyattes (father of the famous King Croesus about whom we will learn in the chapter on Sardis) not only defeated Smyrna in battle, but utterly destroyed it, reducing it to a mere assortment of poor country villages. In ancient times city officials erased the names of deceased residents from its rolls. Strabo writes that Smyrna was stricken from the list of world cities.

Smyrna was dead. Its status as a deceased city lasted four hundred years until one night, while sleeping near a shrine on Mount Pagos, Alexander the Great dreamed of building a new city. Relocated to a fresh water spring about three miles from the rubble of the old, the new Smyrna enjoyed a reputation for being *to agolma tes Asias* – "The Glory of Asia."

The new streets were wide and straight. Apollo, Aphrodite, Asklepios, Cybele, and Zeus had new temples. There was a new civic and a new commercial agora, along with a new grain market. For recreation people went to a new athletic stadium, a new gymnasium, and a new theater with seating for twenty thousand. Those sailing into port through the crystal blue Aegean waters saw the white marble of new public structures glistening like a crown around Mount Pagos, giving credence to the claim on Smyrna's coins that it was "First of Asia in Beauty."

As if resurrected from the grave, the city lived again. Nearly five hundred years later, orators like Aristides still waxed eloquently about Smyrna rising like a phoenix from the ashes.

Except for a section of a Roman street and the ruins of the civic agora, most of the architecture of ancient Smyrna remains hidden, perhaps never to be revealed, covered by the homes and businesses of Turkey's third largest city, Izmir. There are, however, artifacts tastefully displayed in the three buildings of the wonderful new Museum of History and Art – one section dedicated to stone sculptures, a second to ceramics, and a third to precious objects.

Entrance to the ruins of the civic agora is through a gate graced by the sculpted head of Faustina, the wife of Emperor Marcus Aurelius. When informed that the earthquake of 177 CE devastated this most beautiful of cities, the emperor broke into tears, suspended the taxation of Smyrna for ten years, and sent funds for rebuilding.

Today a series of columns stands on the western side of the civic agora, two stories above a succession of supporting arches exposed below ground level. A water channel runs through the arches from the spring of Smyrna, creating respite from the scorching summer heat. Beneath the remains of a

37

three-story basilica (the largest in the Roman world outside Rome) is ancient graffiti – an archaeologist's delight. Skillfully carved column segments, capitals, pedestals, stele, and ossuaries excavated after the moving of an Islamic cemetery are sorted into sections throughout the one hundred thousand square foot courtyard.

The six-pointed star on some ossuaries is a geometric figure from ancient Islamic art – not the Star of David. To date archaeologists have not found a Jewish synagogue, a Jewish quarter, or any distinctly Jewish artifacts in Smyrna. Nevertheless, the literature regarding the second century martyrdom of St. Polycarp, Bishop of Smyrna, along with inscriptions acknowledging monetary gifts from Jewish citizens toward various public projects, confirm the presence of a Jewish population with which, according to Revelation, the church was embroiled in a bitter conflict.

"I know your affliction and your poverty, even though you are rich," the Risen Christ tells John to write to the angel of the church in Smyrna. "I know the slander on the part of those who say that they are Jews and are not, but are a synagogue of Satan."

Given the harsh realities of anti-Semitic bigotry, the horrors of the Holocaust, and the history of hurling Biblical verses as weapons against a people whose covenant with God is not abridged, these words offend modern sensitivities.

Four alternative explanations – none satisfactory – typically are offered for the meaning of the phrase "synagogue of Satan," namely: (1) that the synagogue literally worshiped Satan; (2) that Christianity is the successor to Judaism; (3) that, in keeping with Paul's argument that Jewishness is not defined by ancestry but by faithfulness (Romans 2:28-29), this synagogue must have been unfaithful; and (4) that this synagogue represents some rival Christian group.[25]

A fifth possible explanation is that this synagogue, contrary to the law and the prophets, had women leaders. A plaque found in Smyrna bears the inscription: "Rufina, a Jewess, head of the synagogue, built this tomb for her freed slaves and the slaves raised in her house." According to the Roman Catholic teacher Roland Worth, the argument goes: "It was bad enough that they rejected Jesus; here they were adding insult to injury by flying in the face of a 'universal' Jewish practice." However, the plaque dates to the 2nd century CE, after the writing of Revelation.[26]

---

[25] Worth, Roland H., Jr. *The Seven Cities of the Apocalypse and Greco-Asian Culture*. New York: Paulist Press, 1999. Pages 84-87.

[26] Worth. …*Greco-Asian Culture*. Pages 82-83.

We believe the explanation lies in the first century CE debate regarding whether believers in Jesus formed a sect within Judaism or a separate faith. Initially this debate was internal to the Jewish community. Certainly Jesus and his disciples practiced the Jewish faith, worshipped in the Jewish synagogues, and considered the Jewish law, prophets, and writings as scripture. But the debate intensified as Christianity spread outside Palestine into Roman provinces like Asia where Gentiles believed as well.

Sides formed. As noted in the chapter on Ephesus, the earliest Christian statement of faith was "Jesus is Lord." That faith statement constituted sacrilege to those not recognizing Jesus as the Messiah. At the same time, to those who did, denial of faith in the Risen Christ amounted to blasphemy against the Holy Spirit.

Emperor Domitian's decree that everyone must declare publicly "Caesar is Lord" added fuel to the debate's fire, for it placed Christians on a direct collision course with the Roman state. It also caused those within Judaism not believing in Jesus to want to distance themselves from Christians, lest they risk reprisal from powerful governmental authorities.

Moreover this particular city's famed loyalty to Rome fanned the fire's flames. In 196 BCE, prior to Rome's dominance of the known world, Smyrna became the first city in Asia to build a temple to the goddess Roma. Smyrna was the only city in Asia to send its navy to help the Romans conquer the rest of the Italian peninsula. Smyrna fought side by side with the Romans in the wars against the Seleucids, and its civilians took the clothes off their backs and voluntarily sent them to Roman soldiers shivering in winter battles against the Mithridites. In 26 CE Smyrna became the first city in Asia to win the right to build a temple for the worship of Emperor Tiberius. The loyalty of Smyrna to Rome was so great that Livy proclaimed the city *pro singulari fide* ("singularly faithful"), and Cicero called Smyrna "the city of [Rome's] most faithful and most ancient ally."

In such an atmosphere the pressure to comply with the demands of the Roman state and the Jewish synagogue was immense. Indeed, in the letter to Smyrna the word describing their situation comes straight from the dictionary of torture: *thlipsis*. Translated much too tamely by the English "affliction," it connotes the pressure of being crushed to death by a boulder lowered slowly on one's chest.

Furthermore, failure to comply had additional consequences. The usual Greek word for "poverty" is *penes*, which carries the sense of not having much, not having enough, not having anything extra. By contrast, the word found in this letter is *ptochos*, meaning not having anything at all, to be absolutely destitute.

To this church on the margins of the social order, this congregation subjected to the powerful twin forces of political will and religious establishment, these Christians who had nothing left except the richness of their faith, the Risen Christ pronounces not a single word of criticism. Instead he encourages the Christians in Smyrna for whom it is only going to get worse.

"Do not fear what you are about to suffer," the Risen Christ instructs. "Beware, the devil is about to throw some of you into prison so that you may be tested, and for ten days you will have affliction. Be faithful until death…"

Standing guard at the bottom of the stairs leading from the visitor center to the civic agora is a sculpted lion, mouth open, ready to pounce and devour. Within the civic agora is a chiseled inscription reading:

> To Julius Menecles Diophantus, Asiarch, who has gloriously and zealously presented (a show of combat) with sharpened (weapons) five days successively, his dearest city (pays honour).[27]

Gladiatorial games were initiated under Caesar Augustus, but were not introduced into Asia until 71-70 BCE. Gladiator schools were located in Pergamum, Philadelphia, and here in Smyrna.[28] While there is no evidence of widespread persecution, torture, or killing during the reign of Domitian, shortly afterward the suffering began. Ignatius, the Bishop of Antioch who was born and raised in Smyrna, traveled to Rome and was martyred in 117 CE. Polycarp, whom, according to tradition, John named Bishop of Smyrna in 115 CE through prayer and laying on of hands, was martyred in 156 or 166 CE, along with ten other Christians, some from Philadelphia.

According to that story, word spread through the city that the crowd in the stadium was calling for Polycarp's death. The church in Smyrna hid him on a farm, where Polycarp envisioned being burned alive. Secreted to a second farm, Polycarp continued hiding until betrayed and arrested.

"What harm is there in saying 'Lord Caesar?'" the officer in charge asked as they returned to the city. Polycarp kept silent. In the stadium the Proconsul ordered Polycarp three times to say the loyalty oath. Polycarp's response: "For six and eighty years I have been serving Christ and He has done no wrong to me. How then dare I blaspheme my King who has saved me?" The proconsul warned Polycarp he had wild beasts and fire. Polycarp replied that the proconsul's fire burns for a while, but it is nothing compared to the fire of the second death.

---

[27] Hemer. Page. 69.

[28] Worth. …*Roman Culture*. Pages 26-27.

At that point the herald cried out three times: "Polycarp confesses to being a Christian." The crowd shouted: "This is the teacher of Asia, the father of Christians, the destroyer of our gods!" With the lions already put away for the day, fire became the executioner's tool. Polycarp stood untied on the pyre. When the flames died, like the crucified Jesus' side being pierced with a spear, a dagger punctuated the finality of Polycarp's death.

John knew what happens when faith is misplaced in powerful institutions on a crash course with God. John was aware of the pressure on Christians to compromise with the ways of the world's powerful. When the government, military, corporation, or organized church choose one course of action, and Jesus' teachings lead in the opposite direction, in whom will we place our faith? That is the question raised by this letter. In those who proclaim "Trust us, for we know things you don't," or in the one who claims "I am the way and the truth and the life"?

Contemporary scholar of first century Christianity, John Dominic Crossan, argues that military, economic, political, and ideological power coalesced to create the domination of the Roman Empire, not unlike it does to create the global reach of the United States. Twenty-eight Roman legions, stationed throughout the known world, stood on alert to crush any rebellion, anywhere, anytime. These legions protected the arteries of trade, creating a climate of prosperity complete with a wealthy aristocratic class. Local elites assumed political control, maintaining positions of authority so long as they remained loyal to Rome. And the head of the Roman government assumed not only god-like titles, but also exercised god-like control.

"[T]he imperial program," writes Crossan, "was Romanization by urbanization for commercialization." Power concentrated upward and its maintenance inevitably led to the violence of oppression, poverty, injustice, and persecution. Among the resisters were Jesus and his followers, who countered the paradigm of "first victory, then peace" with a prophetic call to "peace through justice."[29]

While Crossan is not enamored with the book of Revelation, he nevertheless credits John for confronting Christians seduced by what the empire had to offer, acculturated into a value system not of God, and attracted by the trappings of wealth secured by oppression and peace maintained by violence, cooperating – even colluding – with those in power, compromising the faith rather than resisting evil.[30]

---

[29] Crossan, John Dominic. *God and Empire: Jesus Against Rome, Then and Now.* New York: HarperCollins Publishers, 2007. Pages 12-13, 29.

[30] Crossan. Page 222.

Unlike the other letters, there is no condemnation in this one to Smyrna. The Risen Christ recognizes they remain faithful to God, refusing to give into the pressure, living in poverty and being slandered for their stances. But John envisions that physical persecution, even death, will follow as they live out their faith in the public square. So, to the church in Smyrna, a promise is made: even that suffering will not last forever – just ten days.

In the scriptures the number "ten" (or a multiple thereof) typically is used to indicate a great or an infinite amount. During the days of Noah it rained, not for four, but for forty days – a very long time. The people of God wandered in the wilderness for forty years – what felt like forever. When Peter asked if he must forgive another as many as seven times (certainly a magnanimous gesture), Jesus replied not seven but seventy times seven – mercy without end.

By contrast, in this letter the number "ten" functions in the opposite way, indicating a limited or finite period. Such use differs from John's typical pattern of employing the number "three-and-one-half" for an abbreviated period. Some scholars try linking John's use of the number "ten" with the number "five" of the inscription found in Smyrna mentioned previously, projecting that the suffering will be longer than the trials of the gladiatorial games but will not last indefinitely. However, much more likely is that John alludes to the book of Daniel, which begins with a ten-day time of testing.

Daniel is a treatise on civil disobedience, an encouragement to resist those wielding power in this world, and a call to remain singularly faithful to God – an apocalyptic book underscoring John's message in Revelation.

In the opening chapter the world-dominating forces of King Nebuchadnezzar hold Daniel captive. Selected for training in the ways of the Babylonians and ordered to eat and drink from the royal rations, Daniel engages in civil disobedience, refusing to defile himself with unclean foods, consuming only vegetables and water. God sees Daniel through the ten day trial and he is spared the death penalty.

In chapter three, King Nebuchadnezzar commissions the creation of a golden statue and orders everyone in his realm to bow before it. Again Daniel engages in civil disobedience, refusing to worship the idol. Death by fire is the ordered capital punishment. But God sees Daniel though flames intensified seven times normal level, sparing his life.

A third time Daniel is ordered executed for an act of civil disobedience in chapter six. A new king sits on the throne, Darius the Mede, who decrees that no one is to pray to anyone, human or divine, except him. Aware of the law, Daniel nevertheless gets down on his knees three times a day, faces in the direction of Jerusalem, and prays for God's mercy. He does so publicly, in front of an open window, seen from the street. Thrown into the lions' den as punishment, once more God saves Daniel from injury and death.

Like Daniel, the church in Smyrna is not to fear what they are about to face. Rather than to punish criminals, the Romans used prison cells to house short-term the accused pending trial and the convicted awaiting execution. Some in Smyrna will be thrown in prison pending trial. Some will be thrown into prison awaiting their death sentences. Nevertheless, they all have reason to hope. "Be faithful unto death and I will give you the crown of life," the Risen Christ promises; "Whoever conquers will not be harmed by the second death."

Little mystery surrounds the meaning of "the second death." Bruce Metzger, leader of the *New Revised Standard Version's* translation team, writes: "Our first death happens when we take our last breath on earth. The second death comes to impenitent sinners at the Final Judgment."[31] Adds the popular British author/theologian William Barclay: "The second death was a Jewish Rabbinic phrase referring to the total extinction of the utterly wicked."[32]

Often missed in the translation is the double-negative in this promise. In Greek, double-negatives add emphasis. The word "not" should be printed in bold, italicized, capitalized, and underlined! Though those who dare to engage in civil disobedience should expect persecution, there is no reason to fear. Just as no harm came to Daniel in the king's court, in the fiery furnace, or in the lions' dean, in the final judgment the Risen Christ promises no harm for those who resist the powers of evil in the public square. Instead, they will receive "the crown of life."

Two words in Greek can be translated "crown." The first is *diadema*, the royal crown, the symbol of power in a world obsessed with the acquisition of power. The second is *stephanos*, the laurel wreath awarded winning athletes, the festal garland worn at marriage feasts, the emblem of honor given in Smyrna to citizens particularly faithful and loyal in their civic service. The *stephanos* appeared on the coins of Smyrna. *Stephanos* also was the word used in ancient descriptions of the city – the "crown of Smyrna" being a metaphor for the glistening ring of new public buildings surrounding Mt. Pagos' summit.

In Revelation the heavenly courts cast down their golden crowns – *diadema* – before the throne of God, revealing that the power arrangements associated with the *diadema* on earth are not of God. Whatever the pressure brought to bear by powerful personalities and institutions to do something other than

---

[31] Metzger, Bruce M. *Breaking the Code: Understanding the Book of Revelation.* Nashville: Abingdon Press, 1993. Pages 33-34.

[32] Barclay, William. *Letters to the Seven Churches.* Philadelphia: The Westminster Press, 1957. Page 45.

God's will, according to Revelation 4-5, only God and the Lamb upon the throne are worthy to receive the "power and wealth and wisdom and might and honor and glory and blessing" belonging to the *diadema*.

What is promised to the faithful is the crown of joy – the *stephanos* – the crown of life.

> *Let anyone who has an ear listen*
> *to what the Spirit is saying*
> *to the churches.*

5 PERGAMUM

Each day thousands of cars pass Third Church. Sitting in the shadows of three world-renowned institutions, few notice the building except street people hungering for soup and developers salivating over a prime location.

Across the street from the sanctuary is the hospital where extensive medical knowledge, cutting-edge technologies, innovative research techniques, a highly trained staff, genuine art in the hallways, and restaurant quality food create a reputation for first-class care.

The city's main streets converge at the golden dome of the capital building a few blocks east. Powerful politicians, longing lobbyists, nosy reporters, and sign-holding fanatics cross paths, each with an agenda.

To the west about a mile is the university. High up in the library stacks, Sue sits in her study carol, supposedly finishing her dissertation. Instead she stares out the window in the direction of her church.

Sue grew up in the city. What attracted her to Third Church during the Vietnam era was Dr. Dan – an outspoken pastor who preached against that war's immorality. During his ministry the congregation integrated, elected women to leadership positions, and planted trees each Earth Day. Dr. Dan loved Jesus and the prophets. As far as Sue is concerned, his sermons connected with the issues of the day.

Dr. Dan had his public critics. The church's membership never grew. Their building looked old and needed renovation. But none of that used to bother the members. Whenever they had money, they thought it better to help others rather than spend on themselves.

In the years since Dr. Dan's passing a gradual change had come over the church. Members Sue's age questioned less what was going on in the world. Younger members mostly wanted to be "nurtured spiritually," whatever that meant. The pastors following Dr. Dan left Sue with the impression they didn't want to rock the boat by addressing social justice concerns seriously.

Sue recalls the heated debate long ago regarding whether the congregation should remain in the city or relocate to the suburbs. Dr. Dan said they should stay put because they were positioned perfectly to carry out their God-given mission of speaking truth to power and helping the community's poor. His position won the day.

Recently the church received a multi-million dollar offer for their property. Sue can't concentrate. It looks like the vote will go the other way.

2:12 *Write to the angel of the church in Pergamum! Thus saith the one holding the sharp two-edged sword.*

13 *I know where you are living, there where the throne of the adversary is. You are holding up my name. You denied not my faith even in the days of my faithful witness Antipas, who was killed near you where the adversary is living.*

14 *Nevertheless I hold a few things against you: that you have there those supporting the teaching of Balaam, who was instructing Balak to put that which gives occasion for sin before the descendants of Israel, to eat meats sacrificed to idols and to commit sexual immorality.*

15 *In this way you likewise have those supporting the teaching of the Nicolaitans.*

16 *Therefore, repent! Otherwise I am coming to you soon. I will wage war against them with the sword of my mouth.*

17 *Whoever has an ear, hear what the spirit is saying to the churches! To the victor I will give to him/her of the manna that has been hidden. And I will give to her/him a white pebble. Upon the pebble a new name is being written that no one knows except the recipient.*

Rome was the capital of the empire. Pergamum was the capital of the province.

Rome was home to the emperor, supreme ruler of the known world. Pergamum was the residence of his representative, the proconsul, who governed Asia with authority over life and death.

Rome was the epicenter from which the decree went out that Domitian was to be worshipped as *Dominus et Deus* ("Lord and God"). Pergamum was home to the imperial cult, having built a temple to Augustus in 29 BCE, a full century before the one to Domitian in Ephesus.

In John's mind Rome was the personification of evil, a scarlet beast full of blasphemous names, the source of the earth's abominations. In the words of the Risen Christ, Pergamum was the location of "Satan's throne."

Fifty miles northwest of Smyrna and fifteen miles inland from the Aegean Sea, a thirteen hundred foot terraced mountain of gray-blue andesitic stone rises regally over the plain, still beautifully crowned with the ruins of one of the ancient world's most outstanding collections of artistic architectural achievements.

Accessible only from the south by a steep, narrow, hair-pinned road better for someone else to drive, the cool winds of the upper acropolis bring welcome relief from the summer heat of the lower city. The view from above is phenomenal.

Entering from the parking lot, first seen are the remains of four palaces, the grand homes of the Attalids, sovereigns of the Pergamene kingdom, rulers from 281 to 133 BCE. The first palace is the newest; farthest away is the earliest. Just beyond are storage magazines. In front is the Temple to Trajan with its leafy Pergamum-styled columns, built in the second century CE by his successor, Emperor Hadrian.

Not much is left of the famous library, reputed home to two hundred thousand volumes. The dimensions of the three rooms for the stacks plus the reading hall suggest the collection's size is an exaggeration. What can be confirmed is that the walls were double thick and that the shelves hung away from the walls on hooks to protect a substantial number of precious tomes.

So important was this library to the Pergamenes that they attempted a corporate raid on the library personnel in Alexandria, making Aristophanes (the head librarian) a better offer to move to Pergamum. When Ptolemy heard, he threw Aristophanes in jail to ensure he would not leave Egypt, and banned the export of papyrus to Pergamum. In response the people of Pergamum developed a new writing material from animal skins called *Pergamene charta*, from which we get our word "parchment."

In the reading hall stood a second century BCE statue of Athena (modeled after the one at the Parthenon), now found in Berlin at the *Pergamonmuseum*. Also in Berlin is the façade of the Temple to Athena, the oldest Pergamene place of worship. Dating to the fourth century BCE, still standing in line next to the library, are the bases of her sanctuary's columns.

Athena was Pergamum's primary goddess. Athena the Victory-Bearing. She was credited with Pergamum conquering the Gauls, mercenary soldiers from Galatia (central Turkey near Ankara), reputed to be such ferocious warriors that no one could defeat them.

To alleviate his soldiers' fear of the Gauls, King Attalos I of Pergamum offered a sacrifice prior to the battle. Upon inspection for divine messages, the sacrificed animal's liver revealed the words "Victory to the king." Unknown to the king's soldiers was that Attalos wrote those words backward on his hand, imprinting them on the entrails during the sacrifice.

Inside the Temple to Athena were bronze statues celebrating the Pergamene triumph. Roman copies of two of those bronzes – *The Dying Gaul* and *Gaul Killing Himself and Wife* – are in Rome's *Museo Capitolino* and *Museo Nazionale delle Terme* respectively.

On the mountainside in front and below this temple, with seating for ten thousand in eighty rows, is the steepest theater in Asia, seats cut from native andesite, except for the king's marble box. Actors performed on a portable wooden stage placed atop the square stones with holes still visible from above. Near the theater is the Temple to Dionysus, whose priests rolled out an altar prior to each performance for the offering of libations to the theater's god.

On the terrace above the theater and near the Temple to Athena are five rows of steps circumnavigating an area one-hundred nineteen feet wide by one-hundred twelve feet deep. Here stood the altar to this city's other primary god: Zeus, the greatest of the Olympian gods, the god the Pergamenes called "Savior."

The horseshoe-shaped altar (also on view in Berlin) is forty feet high, surrounded by nearly four hundred linear feet of life-sized sculpted friezes which only can be described as awesome. A sixty-five foot wide flight of stairs ascends to an open surface. Some scholars wonder if the sacrifices offered on this great altar were to Athena as well as Zeus.

The sculptures depict the ancient myth of the battle between the gods and the giants. Nearly all the major Olympian gods are portrayed around the altar – not only Zeus and Athena but also Aphrodite, Apollo, Ares, Artemis, Dionysus, Hermes, Hephaestus, Poseidon, etc. A host of minor Greek gods fight side-by-side with them. Their enemies are a slew of giants, powerful beings wrecking havoc on earth, born clad in armor with spears in hand, legs scaled like dragons, with the tails of snakes.

On the frieze is a single mortal. According to the myth, the outcome of the battle between the gods and the giants lies in question until a human being decides to side with good rather than evil. The mortal who does is Heracles.

To the Greeks this myth portrayed the superiority of rationality. The faces of the gods show no emotion. The giants' faces contort with anguish and fear.

To the Pergamenes this monument celebrated their victory over the Gauls – their conquering, with the help of the gods, an otherwise invincible menacing military giant.

To John this altar represented everything demonic. Seeing the dragon scales and the serpents' tails, John would have agreed evil is gigantic in proportion. Viewing Heracles, he would have affirmed human beings must choose a side. However, to John, the war waged both on earth and in the spiritual realm was not between the gods and the giants, but between God and the gods. John heard the Risen Christ calling the seven churches – commanding the church on earth – to join the hosts of heaven in that battle.

In Pergamum's lower city, at the medical center, another prominent god was worshipped. This god's symbol was the caduceus – a rod entwined with snakes – associated to this day with the field of medicine. The god's name was Asclepios.

Pergamum was the Lourdes of Asia. People journeyed to the hospital there like we travel to Mayo, Sloan-Kettering, John Hopkins, or the Cleveland Clinic. Most of the ruins date to the second century CE. This hospital's most famous physician, Galen, was a surgeon to the gladiators who lived in the second century BCE. Diseases of the digestive track were the staff's specialty, particularly ailments of the stomach, bowels, and intestines.

Well ahead of their time, this medical staff believed in treating the whole person – body, mind, and spirit. They emphasized the value of exercise, diet, and rest. So those in their care might be stimulated by music, drama, and literature, they built a library and a small theater seating thirty-five hundred, where they held poetry contests, concerts, and plays.

The hospital slept forty male and seventeen female patients. Upon admission patients walked down a long tunnel to a round treatment center where they moved around the circle visiting the offices of various doctors for examination and diagnosis. Tour guides today say the square openings in tunnel's roof allowed in not only sunlight and fresh air but also the voices of the hospital's personnel repeating "You are going to get better. You are going to get better. You are going to get better..." One would like to believe that is true.

This medical complex had a chapel – a round building dedicated to Asclepios. In the temple courtyard to this day stands a round altar to the Greek god of healing, covered with sculpted snakes. Snakes are associated with the medical field because they shed their old skins, thus appearing to gain renewed and healthy bodies. Some say one large snake was caged in this temple; others report that several snakes slithered freely. Patients slept on the temple's floor, hoping for a miraculous healing. Believing Asclepios to be a god who visited mortals during night-visions, the doctors encouraged patients to participate in their own healing by sharing their dreams for proper interpretation and incorporation into treatment plans.

Pergamum was a city of prominence. (In John's time) it was the governmental capital of Asia, the center of the imperial cult in Asia, the location of the most famous library in Asia, the site of sculpture unmatched in Asia, and home to the most advanced medical complex in Asia. Ephesus was the "Supreme Metropolis of Asia." Smyrna was the "Most Beautiful City in Asia." Pergamum was the "First City in Asia" – not first as in earliest, but first as in best.

But why? This out-of-the-way place was not a port, not located on a major trade route, and not mentioned in any literature earlier than *Anabasis*, the journal a Greek mercenary named Xenophon kept while returning from the Persian wars. A single reference to Pergamum marks it as the spot where, in 399 BCE, the soldier met a Spartan commander who won one of the Peloponnesian Wars against the Athenians. Understanding requires working through a little more history, which is much more complicated.

Upon his premature death in 323 BCE, the empire of Alexander the Great was partitioned between four generals. A conflict arose between two, Antigonus and Seleucus, over the land that is now western Turkey. A third general, Lysimachus, sided with the Seleucid forces which defeated the Antigonid army in 301 BCE. Pergamum was among the spoils of war given to Lysimachus, who appointed a mercenary soldier named Philetairos as its local governor, funding him with a substantial treasury totaling nine thousand talents.

When the Seleucids killed Lysimachus in battle twenty years later, Philateiros inherited the city and its treasury, established his own small kingdom, and used the money to beautify the city with public buildings and temples to various Greek gods, in the hope of assuring the Seleucids that even if Lysimachus turned on them, he would not.

Following Philateiros (281-263 BCE) was a one-hundred thirty year period of Pergamene kings named either Eumenes or Attalos. Eumenes I (263-241 BCE), wanting to establish the city's independence by expanding the kingdom's borders, entered an alliance with the Egyptians to defeat the Seleucids near Sardis in 262 BCE. Throughout the long reign of his adopted son Attolos I (241-197 BCE), not only were the Seleucids held off, but so were the Gauls.

When the Roman armies marched on Asia during the reign of Eumenes II (197-159 BCE), Pergemene soldiers fought side-by-side with the Romans to defeat the Seleucids once and for all. Dubbed a hero for defeating the armored Persian cavalry in the Seleucid ranks, Eumenes II received much of the Seleucid territory, as well as the right to collect from all the cities which previously paid tribute to the Seleucids.

Eumenes II used those funds atop the acropolis to fortify the citadel, erect the monuments, commission the sculptures, establish the world-class library, build the temples, construct the public buildings – in short, to make

Pergamum the premiere city, the envy of every other Hellenistic city, the "First City in Asia."

While the successor to Eumenes II, Attalos II (159-138 BCE), worked hard at doing nothing to offend the Romans, the next (and last) king, Attalos III (138-133 BCE), did nothing to help Pergamum remain independent. Instead he gave the kingdom to the Romans in his will.

"And to the angel of the church in Pergamum write: These are the words of him who has the sharp two-edged sword."

Along with sculptures, coins, and jewelry, the museums throughout Turkey display weaponry. On exhibit are different types of swords from short plain daggers to long bejeweled gifts, heavy broad sabers to curved oriental scimitars, singled-edged Greek cutting instruments to the thrusting ones of the Roman legions.

The "sharp two-edged sword" was rare in the first century. Reserved for Roman officials of the highest rank, it symbolized the authority bestowed upon the few vested with *jus gladdi* (the "right of the sword"), who alone could render capital punishment. In their offices, literally, was the power of life and death. In the province of Asia, it was worn only by the Roman proconsul living in Pergamum.

This third letter boldly declares that, contrary to common knowledge, power and authority over life and death belong not to the proconsul but to the Risen Christ. "From his mouth," John reminds the Christians in Pergamum of the vision recorded in Revelation's first chapter, "came a sharp two-edged sword."

That this particular type of sword is in his mouth reflects the prophetic understanding that whatever God says, whatever content follows "Thus saith the Lord...," whatever words the Pergamenes hear from the lips of the Risen Christ are ultimate and decisive. As the unnamed author of Hebrews 4:12-13 put it a generation later:

> Indeed, the word of God is living and active, sharper than any two-edged sword, piercing until it divides soul from spirit, joints from marrow; it is able to judge the thoughts and intentions of the heart. And before him no creature is hidden, but all are naked and laid bare to the eyes of the one to whom we must render an account.

"I know where you are living," begins the Risen Christ, "where Satan's throne is." The referent for "Satan's throne" is a matter of much debate.

Given the title for the Risen Christ beginning this third letter, some believe "Satan" refers to the Roman Empire and "throne" to Pergamum being the seat of Roman command throughout the province. After all Pergamum was the Roman capital of Asia, the center of the Roman imperial cult in Asia, the headquarters for Roman rule over Asia as incarnated in the proconsul. Throughout Revelation, John consistently associates everything regarding Rome with evil.

Others point to the sheer number of temples, altars, and sculptures dominating the landscape, dedicated not just to the imperial cult but to an array of goddesses and gods. When Eumenes II undertook his grand building plan, he wanted Pergamum to be the Athens of Asia. Like Paul on Mars Hill, John sees a city filled with idols to false gods. Accordingly, these commentators argue, the city of Pergamum as a whole must be "Satan's throne."

Noting the equation between evil and the serpent dating to the story of Adam and Eve (a linkage John explicitly makes in Revelation when he writes of "the dragon, that ancient serpent, who is the Devil and Satan"), other commentators make the case that "Satan's throne" is a specific reference to the cult of Asclepios, to that famous medical complex, to the god of healing whose symbol is the snake. Even the Pergemene coins bore the images of snakes.

Certainly there are times when that particular god competes successfully for devotion in today's world. How much of an exaggeration is it to say that in Western society the architecture of modern hospitals replaces medieval cathedrals; that people look to pills, surgery, and therapy to provide health, hope, and happiness; that physicians rather than God are more likely thanked for giving life, more life, and more quality in life?

This is not to imply medical treatment is not of value. It is to say the medical establishment doesn't cure anyone. Rather, it facilitates the healing process originating with God who blesses the medical profession with education, facilities, skills, staffs, technologies, and other resources though which God acts. John would not have us confused regarding who should receive the glory.

While this last case for understanding "Satan's throne" is stronger than the first two, there is a fourth possibility, namely that those receiving the letter to Pergamum most naturally associated "Satan's throne" with the altar to Zeus.

We find this interpretation most compelling not only because virtually every major god in the Greco-Roman world appears somewhere on that altar; not only because the giants on that altar, representing evil forces roaming the face of the earth, are depicted with serpent tails and are covered by dragon scales; not only because, observing the mountain's profile from a distance, the terrace on which that altar stood appears like the seat of a gigantic chair; but also because the aroma of sacrifices burned on that altar hovered continually over the Pergemene populace, permeating the air like the smell of chocolate encompasses Hersey, Pennsylvania, or, with respect to John's nostrils, like the stench of the steel mills that once caused the region southeast of Chicago to stink.

"I know where you are living," the Risen Christ continues. Two Greek words may be translated as "living." The first, *paroikein*, denotes a temporary address; the second, *katoikein*, connotes a permanent residence. The second is used in this letter.

The Risen Christ knows Christians in Pergamum live, work, and socialize in the constant odor of meat offered to idols descending from that altar. They cannot escape it. Despite the advantages of life in the first, the best, the capital city of Asia, where they live reeks with evil. In the battle between God and the gods, they must deal with the evil where they live.

"Yet you are holding fast to my name, and you did not deny your faith in me even in the days of Antipas my witness, my faithful one, who was killed among you, where Satan lives." While the persecution of Christians during Domitian's reign was not extensive as once believed, this verse suggests an incident did occur in Pergamum. The verbs "deny" and "kill" are in the aorist tense, indicating the martyrdom of a single individual at a particular point in time, about whom we know nothing.

Did the Roman proconsul decide to make Antipas an example of what would follow should other Christians prove troublesome? Perhaps. Certainly having even one member of their congregation killed for the faith would have caused others to pause and question how much of a witness they were willing to make.

However, if so, that frightening time evidently did not have the intended dampening effect. The first verb in the verse is in the present tense. As John writes Revelation, this church is lifting up the name of Jesus rather than capitulating to Caesar's decree. The Risen Christ commends them for that, encouraging them in their daily struggle against evil by bestowing upon Antipas the title "faithful witness" – a description of the Risen Christ found in Revelation 1.

At the same time the church in Pergamum is not beyond criticism. "But I have a few things against you," the Risen Christ continues; " you have some there who hold to the teaching of Balaam, who taught Balak to put a stumbling block before the people of Israel, so that they would eat food sacrificed to idols and practice fornication. So you also have some who hold to the teaching of the Nicolaitans."

The story of Balaam and Balak is told in Numbers. While that Biblical book largely is forgotten by the contemporary church, this particular story is famous for its talking donkey.

Balaam is a prophet of God. Balak is the king of Moab. According to the story, Balak is willing to pay Balaam to curse God's people who, having escaped from Egypt in their journey toward the Promised Land, now have arrived on the plains of Moab. Balak's concern: there are so many of them! He fears the sheer number of Hebrew people will overrun the Moabites.

After sleeping on the request, Balaam sends the first delegation back to Balak saying it isn't God's will for him to do what the king wants. When a second – more prestigious – delegation is sent, Balaam first tells them they cannot pay him enough to go against God's will, but then decides maybe it is God's will for him to honor Balak's request after all. So he sets out on his donkey toward Moab. God is not pleased.

Three times along the way the donkey sees what Balaam does not: the angel of the Lord, sword in hand, blocking the way. Is it a sharp two-edged sword? The first time the donkey veers off the road. The second time he scraps Balaam's foot against a wall. The third time he drops in his tracks, refusing to budge. Each time Balaam beats the donkey with a stick, until finally the donkey turns to the prophet and asks, in effect: "Why are you hitting me? Have I ever done anything wrong to you before? What makes you think I'm not doing what is in your best interest now?" Balaam admits he has been a good donkey, at which point the prophet's eyes are opened and he, too, sees the angel blocking his way.

The angel tells Balaam God is not happy with this trip. Balaam offers to turn around and go home, but continues on anyway, warned he better do what God wills or else.

While in Moab, Balaam is taken to see the Hebrew encampment in the distance, offers sacrifices to determine God's will, and does precisely the opposite of what Balak is paying him to do. He blesses the people of God rather than curse them. At least that is the earliest edition of the story as recorded in Numbers 22-24.

Numbers contains traces of different versions of the same stories compiled from several traditions, geographical regions, and time periods. Contrary to considering Balaam an advocate for God's will who resists the pressure to curse what God wants blessed, the priestly tradition blames Balaam in Numbers 25 and 31 for causing great unfaithfulness, chastises him for placing a stumbling block before God's people, and holds him responsible for Hebrew men marrying Moabite women, being seduced by them into worshipping other gods, and eating meat offered to idols. John embraces this later negative tradition.

The meat from the sacrifices offered on the altar to Zeus, along with the meat sacrificed on the altars of other temples in Pergamum, was the same meat served at banquets, the same meat for sale at the agora, the same meat available in restaurants, and the same meat brought to potlucks. For that reason, the issue of whether Christians could eat meat offered to idols was a live question in the first century, one over which Paul and John disagree somewhat.

First Corinthians 8 opens by arguing that since there is no god but God, meat offered to idols is just meat, eating it is of no consequence, and Christians are free to consume it unless doing so would create a problem for someone who does not know as much about the true nature of God. By the end of that chapter, however, as a practical matter, Paul reveals he personally refuses to eat it.

John, in the letter to Pergamum as well as in the next letter to Thyatira, argues that because gods and goddesses represent dangerous spiritual realities, they have the power to lure Christians away from God by what they appear to offer, and therefore any eating of meat offered to idols represents unfaithfulness.

These contrasting theological positions stand as correctives – Paul emphasizing Christian liberty and John underscoring human sinfulness.

Coupled with the admonition not to eat food offered to idols is another not to practice fornication. Both appear as well in the heated debate of the Council of Jerusalem described in Acts 15.

According to the story, the apostles and the elders of the first century church gather in Jerusalem to settle the fight over whether Gentiles need to become Jewish in order to be Christian. Some are adamant God's law requires circumcision. Paul considers circumcision a needless impediment to his missionary efforts. This dispute, according to Luke, created "no small dissention and debate."

After hearing from Peter why he has changed his mind on the issue, as well as listening to testimonies from Paul and Barnabas about the miraculous work God has been doing on the frontier, James (the brother of Jesus) renders the Council's decision. Circumcision will not be allowed to serve as a stumbling block for people turning to God; however, not eating food offered to idols and refraining from practicing fornication (along with a couple other things) still are expected.

The word "fornication" in the scriptures may be interpreted literally as "sexual immorality" or metaphorically as "religious unfaithfulness." The prophets commonly used the word in the later sense as the reason for God's people being sent into the Babylonian captivity. John consistently uses the word in Revelation either in the context of people seduced by the power, glory, and wealth of the Roman Empire, or in relation to their giving in to the temptation to worship a false god.

Unfaithfulness to God is John's biggest concern. John wants the Christian church to take on what is not of God in this world, even as the angels are fighting the same battle in the spiritual realm. The very last thing John wants is for the church to compromise, to capitulate to evil, to be conquered by it.

In the chapter on Ephesians we observed that "Nicolaitans" is derived from two Greek words: *nikan* meaning "to conquer" and *laos* meaning "the people." Fascinatingly, the name "Balaam" is derived from two Hebrew words: *baal* meaning "to conquer" and *ha'am* meaning "the people."

Evidently within the church in Pergamum, as in Ephesus, there were Christians causing other Christians to stumble and be conquered by the false gods and goddesses of the world, rather than be empowered to stand tall and witness for the faith like Antipas. The Risen Christ's single instruction: "Repent then." Unlike Balaam, they are not to tolerate what is less than God's will and cause another to become unfaithful.

"If not," warns the Risen Christ, "I will come to you soon and make war against them with the sword of my mouth." The pronouns in this verse are confusing unless one remembers the "you" in all seven letters is singular and refers to the angel. The Risen Christ is addressing the spirit, the ethos, the essence of each church. The church in Pergamum is warned that if it does not change course by addressing its congregational tendency to compromise with evil, at some future date the Risen Christ will use his power and authority to vanquish the congregation.

Then comes the Risen Christ's promise: "To everyone who conquers" – to all who are faithful and do not cause others to become unfaithful – "I will give some of the hidden manna, and I will give a white stone, and on the white stone is written a new name that no one knows except the one who receives it."

While Pergamum's medical establishment associated the word "manna" with the frankincense used to treat nosebleeds and eyesores, in this verse it connects to an ancient Jewish tradition not recorded in Hebrew scripture, holding that in addition to the stone tablets of the Ten Commandments and to Aaron's robe, kept in the Jerusalem Temple's Holy of Holies was a pot filled with the food God provided God's people in the wilderness. Hidden by the prophet Jeremiah at the time of the Temple's destruction, it was believed this pot of hidden manna would reappear when the Messiah arrived.

The appearance of the Risen Christ offering manna to the church in Pergamum stands in stark contrast with a congregation eating food offered to idols. The first is a sign of God's faithfulness; the second is an act of human infidelity.

The Risen Christ also promises a white stone. Theories regarding the meaning are numerous, speculative, and unsatisfying. While the Greek *psephos* suggests a round stone worn smooth by water or polish, most potential referents are tesserae – six-sided dice-like cubes used in mosaics.[33]

Commentators suggest linkages ranging from coupons for free bread to tickets for entertainment events, to good luck charms, to votes for acquittal by juries, to a symbol for a happy day (as in Pliny talking of a day "marked by

---

[33] Worth. …*Greco-Asian Culture*. Page 143.

the whitest of white stones"), to marble pillars in the medical complex bearing the names of people who had been cured, to a prize awarded gladiators.

The last is intriguing. Gladiators surviving their first three years of fighting enjoyed the privilege of refusing matches. They received their freedom if they fought and lived for five years. In some parts of the Roman world, upon retiring from the arena, gladiators received a white stone with the letters "SP" inscribed on the back, an abbreviation of the word *spectatus*, meaning "tried and proved." However, no such artifact has been found in Asia.

The most common theory is that the white stone refers to an amulet with secret writing believed to bring protection against evil. This appears a tempting option until one remembers Antipas was martyred. Christians are called to engage in the gigantic struggle against evil; but the Risen Christ provides no magical guarantee of personal safety during the fight.

Several scriptural stories speak of a new name signaling a changed reality. Abram becomes Abraham and Sarai becomes Sarah when God covenants to give them a child in their old age. Jacob becomes Israel after spending a night wrestling with God. Simon becomes Peter when he confesses Jesus is the Christ. Saul becomes Paul after God's light blinded him on the Damascus Road. Even Antipas of Pergamum receives a new name – "my faithful witness" – upon martyrdom.

But why did the Risen Christ promise this congregation that if they repent, if their corporate life takes a different direction, if they change from a partial to a fully faithful witness, they will receive a secret new name?

The answer may lie in the ancient belief that to name or to know the name is to have power. Adam exercises dominion over the animals by naming them. When Moses asks for God's name, he is not given it for no one is allowed power over God. The essence of this concept is echoed today by consultants who know that being able "to name the name" of what ails, what is problematical, or what is unjust, empowers a person to recover, to solve, or to right a wrong. It is as if the Risen Christ is assuring them that in the battle between God and the gods, the God who knows them by name will not allow the gods and goddess of this world to have final power and authority over them.

In the second volume of his trilogy, *Naming the Powers*, Wink, writes:

> Satan is not "behind" the scenes scheming up idolatry and iniquity. Satan is manifested in idolatry, in iniquity, in the darkness of unbelief and defilement... "Satan's throne" is not in heaven or the lower firmament but on the Acropolis at Pergamum... The threat is not from the sky but from yon sacred hill, not from a malevolent universe bent on their undoing but from the local markets that sell sacrificed meats.

For the Seer of the Apocalypse, the satanic is not an abstract force... It is the concentrated inner spirituality of idolatrous human structures.[34]

**Let anyone who has an ear listen
to what the Spirit is saying
to the churches.**

Ionic
Corinthian
pergamum

Asklepion
(med. doctors & medicine
in this area) clinic

This was a very prominent
city — city of Asia — leading

Turkey

---

[34] Wink, Walter. *Naming the Powers: The Language of Power in the New Testament*. Philadelphia: Fortress Press, 1984. Page 139.

6 THYATIRA

Hard hat tilted back, empty lunch bucket in hand, Jack glances at the overhead crane before heading out the door. The blast furnace takes no break for the shift change. Sparks rain from the oversized bucket as molten iron pours down long narrow molds. Ever since the discovery of ore lured Jack's ancestors to the area, his extended family has worked in the mill. It's dirty work. At least it's honest.

Something dishonest is happening at Jack's church. It's tearing up the congregation, his family, and his insides.

Fourth Church is located in a working community of local shops and specialty factories. There is nothing pretty or pretentious about the town – just a dot on the map. No one would plan to vacation there. But it is Jack's home – home for family reunions and picnics in the park, Main Street parades and Little League baseball, ice cream socials and Sunday morning services.

The brick exterior recently pointed and tucked suggests the members take care of their church building. With a soup kitchen and thrift closet, Fourth Church is known in the community as a place that cares for the least of these. But the glue holding Fourth Church together consists of the caring relationships the members enjoy with one another. Everyone knows everyone else's story – each one's hopes and dreams, aches and pains, failures and achievements. They have supported each other through good times and bad. "That kind of caring is worth something," Jack thinks to himself, climbing into his car. "We cannot lose that."

But Jack knows they can...and they are. A conflict has erupted and families are leaving. Gone already are Jack's daughter, her husband, and the grandkids.

Several months ago a couple new families moved to town. They attended church regularly and their children joined the youth group. Before long they were singing in the choir and volunteering for committees. Fourth Church welcomed them with open arms.

But then, quietly at first, the nit-picking began. Over coffee these new families started putting down the pastor, saying he didn't call enough and wasn't much of a preacher. It got worse soon after. They said he was preaching his own opinions instead of the word of God; that his seminary was suspect for its left-leaning professors; and that the denomination was leading people astray. Seeds of discontent began sprouting where they shouldn't have grown. The regional church office tried helping, but that meeting got ugly.

"Our church never acted like that before," Jack mumbles to himself. He's still embarrassed for not speaking up to defend the pastor. He ponders: "Perhaps we long-timers have become too nice." But he isn't sure. He just knows he wants the conflict to go away, for people to get along, for the church family to make peace.

As Jack reaches home another troubling thought crosses his mind. He doesn't like even thinking it. "If these new families ever get control of the endowment," he dares to say the words aloud, "Mom and Dad are going to turn over in their graves."

Arriving home, Jack showers, eats supper, and sits for the evening in his overstuffed chair. He turns on the table lamp and begins reading the paperback the regional church officer left the night of the blowup. It's about something called "steeplejacking."[35]

2:18 *Write to the angel of the church in Thyatira! Thus saith the son of God, the one whose eyes are like a fiery flame, and whose feet resemble fine bronze.*

19 *I know your accomplishments and love and faith and service and your patience. Your latest works surpass the first.*

20 *Nevertheless, I hold against you that you are tolerating the woman Jezebel, the one calling herself a prophetess, and she is teaching and misleading my servants to commit sexual immorality and to eat meats offered to idols.*

---

[35] See Culver, Sheldon and John Dorhauer. *Steeplejacking: How the Christian Right is Hijacking Mainstream Religion.* New York: Ig Publishing, 2007.

²¹I gave her time so that she might have a change of heart, but she is not willing to repent of her sexual immorality.

²²Listen! I am throwing her onto a feasting couch, and those committing adultery with her into great suffering, unless they turn away from her doings.

²³I will strike her children dead, and all the churches will know for themselves that I am the one searching minds and hearts. I will give to each of you according to your doings.

²⁴Yet I am saying to you, to the remaining ones in Thyatira, as many as are not keeping this teaching, whoever knew not what they call "the depths" of the adversary: I am not casting upon you another burden.

²⁵Just hold fast to what you have until I come!

²⁶The victor and the keeper of my works until the end, I will give to him/her authority over the nations; ²⁷and s/he will rule them with an iron staff, as the vessels belonging to the potters are broken, ²⁸and even as I have received from my father, I will give to her/him the morning star.

²⁹Whoever has an ear, hear what the spirit is saying to the churches!

Thyatira is the longest letter of the seven, and the easiest one in which to get sidetracked. It also is the city with the fewest archeological ruins and the least distinguished history.

Thyatira's archaeological park is in the downtown shopping district, surrounded by busy streets and insufficient parking. No need to buy a ticket. The ruins are viewed easily from the sidewalk through a wrought-iron fence.

A marble portico once marked the western entrance to an ancient colonnaded boulevard. Now its second century columns and capitals, along with a couple fourth century arches, lie strewn about the grounds. The apse of a fifth or sixth century basilica has yielded no religious artifacts, suggesting the facility was civic.

That is all. Further digging appears unlikely. Yet having so little remain seems appropriate for a town the Roman historian, Pliny the Elder, put at the top of his list of "unimportant communities."[36]

According to John's contemporary, Pliny the Younger, the city was founded by the Lydians, who called it Pelopia.[37] The Lydian Empire existed no earlier than the eighth century BCE and eventually encompassed most of Asia Minor. Its capital was Sardis, twenty-five miles to the south. Located in a fertile valley with gently rolling hills but no natural defenses, Pelopia was vulnerable to attack and predictably changed hands with successive invasions.

When Alexander the Great's empire was partitioned between his four generals in 323 BCE, Pelopia went to Seleucus. He renamed it Thyatira and stationed Macedonian troops there. Though no evidence of a Jewish population has been unearthed to date, according to Josephus, Seleucus moved a Jewish colony to Thyatira, presumably to turn this military outpost into a more settled community.[38] But when a rival general was given Pergamum forty-five miles to the north, Thyatira became a border town ping-ponging between the two powers, finally landing in Pergamum's court in 189 BCE.

While Pergamum strengthened the military presence in the city, with no natural protection Thyatira remained essentially a defenseless outpost. The soldiers' primary mission was to hold out against invaders as long as possible, buying time for the troops back in Pergamum to mount a proper defense of the capital.

The last Pergamene king, Attalos III, willed Thyatira to the Romans in the 130s BCE.

Thyatira is mentioned elsewhere in the scriptures only in Acts 16, where Paul encountered, baptized, and stayed in the home of Lydia. Originally from Thyatira, Lydia lived in Philippi, selling purple cloth. Engineered from the madder root or the murex shellfish, Thyatira's purple dye was more reddish than bluish. Pliny the Elder writes that a single pound of the purple dye cost one-thousand denarii – a denarius being a full day's pay for a full day's work.[39] No wonder purple was the color reserved for the rich and the powerful! According to Worth, "the Roman government exercised a monopoly on

---

[36] Barclay. Pages 64.

[37] Blake, Everett C. and Anna G. Edmonds. *Biblical Sites in Turkey*. Istanbul: SEV Matbaacilik ve, Yayincilik, 1997. Page 131.

[38] Blake and Edmonds. Page 132.

[39] Barclay. Pages 65-66.

purple beginning with Nero's reign (if not earlier)... [implying that Lydia's] business inevitably required a connection with the imperial regime."[40]

There are no stories of famous poets or philosophers, historians or athletes, government officials or religious leaders associated with the city. No one writes of any earth-changing or earth-shattering events. But there are artifacts indicating Thyatira was populated by artisans and apprentices. Inscriptions "mention guilds of woolworkers, linen workers, makers of outer garments, dyers, leatherworkers, tanners, potters, bakers, slave dealers, and bronze smiths."[41]

The guilds drew together persons with similar interests and concerns, from owners to employees to slaves, providing the basis for their social life. The guilds in Thyatira were licensed by the Roman government. They claimed the city's god – Tryimnaios Pythoios Apollo – as their divine patron and provider.[42]

The letter to Thyatira begins: "And to the angel of the church in Thyatira write: These are the words of the Son of God, who has eyes like a flame of fire, and whose feet are like burnished bronze."

The title "Son of God" does not appear in Revelation 1 where "Son of Man" is used instead. Nor is the title found anywhere else in Revelation. As if reserved for this letter, the title counters the city's primary god, who was believed to be the son of Zeus. The city's coins depicted Apollos as a sun god, sporting a long cloak and carrying a battle-axe.[43] John would not have the church confused about who rightfully bears the title.

"Fiery eyes" and "burnished bronze" are found in the opening chapter's description of the Risen Christ. They allude to a vision in Daniel 10 where the prophet sees one whose "eyes [are] like flaming torches," and whose "arms and legs [are] like the gleam of burnished bronze," and whose "words [are] like the roar of a multitude." At the sound of the words, Daniel falls face to the ground, lies prostrate, and listens. It is the posture of submission John wants the church in Thyatira to assume relative to the divine message it is about to receive.

"Fiery" suggests intensity – angry eyes, penetrating to the core, missing nothing, not liking what they see.

---

[40] Worth. ...*Greco-Asian Culture*. Page 158

[41] Metzger. Page 36.

[42] Worth. ...*Greco-Asian Culture*... Pages 155-157.

[43] Blake and Edmonds, Page 131.

The word translated "burnished bronze" – *chalkolibanon* – appears only here in the New Testament. Perhaps its use suggests the bronze fired in Thyatira's furnaces was of singularly fine quality. Certainly it underscores the intimate knowledge John and the Risen Christ have of the city. They speak the language of the bronze smiths.

"I know your works – your love, faith, service, and patient endurance. I know that your last works are greater than the first." The letter's praise section is abbreviated, especially compared to the pointed criticism and warning following. Because all the Greek terms are the usual ones – agape for "love," *pistis* for "faith," *diakonia* for "service," *hupomone* for "patient endurance," and *ergon* for "work" – there are no nuances requiring expansive explanation. Together they describe a healthy church engaged in a solid mission.

Nevertheless there is a problem in Thyatira. "But I have this against you: you tolerate that woman Jezebel, who calls herself a prophet..."

As I write this chapter I am at the home of our youngest son and daughter-in-law, who are expecting their first child. On their kitchen counter lies a book of children's names. Some names are so culturally connected with certain individuals, the book cautions, that "the association is something you must make peace with before choosing the name for your child."[44] With respect to the name "Jezebel," there is an understatement! Jezebel makes the book's list of names to be avoided, as the evil queen in First and Second Kings, Ahab's Phoenician wife who promoted pagan worship throughout Israel, the powerful enemy of two of God's greatest prophets.

What raised the ire of Elijah and Elisha was that the original Queen Jezebel used her privileged position to promote the worship of foreign gods. She used her great wealth to support four hundred fifty prophets of Baal and four hundred prophets of Asherah. She viciously opposed the prophets of God who decreed that her influence no longer could be tolerated.

The displeasure of the Risen Christ is roused, in part, because one self-appointed person in Thyatira claims to speak for God. Unable or unwilling to see the harm she is causing, she considers herself a prophet. Few would make such a claim today, at least not aloud. But there are individuals who speak and act as if they are self-declared messengers from God. Quick to quote scripture, they are quicker still to demand their way until they get it.

John's protagonist is leading a portion of the church astray. She is "teaching and beguiling my servants to practice fornication and to eat food sacrificed to idols," the Risen Christ asserts. "I gave her time to repent, but she refuses to repent of her fornication."

---

[44] Wattenberg, Laura. *The Baby Name Wizard: A Magical Method for Finding the Perfect Name for Your Baby.* New York: Broadway Books, 2005. Page 263.

Please see the chapter on Pergamum for an explanation of "fornication" and "food offered to idols" as metaphors for spiritual unfaithfulness. The second metaphor would have been particularly powerful in a town where guilds had their own halls and gods.

Certainly John takes issue with the false prophet and those who follow her. But what we must not overlook is that his primary concern is not with Jezebel, but with a church that will not confront her, which refuses to challenge her teachings. Even those who do not believe a word she says still are providing her with a platform for what is not of God. The congregation's conflict avoidance behavior serves only to promote her misleading. It is enough to make the eyes of the Risen Christ see red: "But I have this against you: you tolerate…"

Commentators commonly point to the parallels between Pergamum and Thyatira (the false prophets, and the metaphors of "food offered to idols" and "fornication"), but they tend to miss the Thyatira-Ephesus connection. The first church and the fourth have opposite problems with the same issue. Ephesus tolerates too little. Thyatira tolerates too much. The church in Ephesus is so intolerant of false prophets and false teachings that it has forgotten what it means to love. The church in Thyatira is so accepting that it tolerates what it should not.

If the letter from the Risen Christ to the church in Ephesus is an indictment against the hard-heartedness of rigid fundamentalism, then the letter to the church in Thyatira brings charges against the soft-mindedness of indiscriminate progressivism. Hospitality does have its boundary at the point where the Body of Christ is harmed rather than built up. Openness to other perspectives does have it limits, for everyone's opinions are not equally valid, nor are everyone's theological understandings sound.

Certainly there is no toleration in the warning section of the letter: "Beware, I am throwing her on a bed, and those who commit adultery with her I am throwing into great distress, unless they repent of her doings; and I will strike her children dead."

The punishment is of the same spirit as the final demise of the original Queen Jezebel who, after applying make-up to her eyes and fixing up her hair, was thrown out a window, her blood splattering on the palace walls, her body trampled by horses, and all but her skull, palms, and feet eaten by dogs.

Proper understanding of the word "bed" may keep us from getting sidetracked into too much gratuitous sex and violence. The Greek word is *kline*. We are told those who crawl into bed with the false prophet will experience "great distress." So, is it a lover's bed? Or is it a sick bed? Or could it be a funeral bier?

Actually, there is no reason to go beyond the usual definition: "feasting couch." In ancient times, the *kline* was the bed on which diners reclined while leisurely consuming the evening meal. Linguistically, a sexualize context for a word associated with eating emphasizes John's prophetic focus on spiritual unfaithfulness. The warning is that God is not as tolerant as Thyatira with respect to those who "refuse to repent."

Once God's sentence against the false prophet and her followers is carried out, declares the Risen Christ, "All the churches will know that I am the one who searches minds and hearts, and I will give to each of you as your works deserve."

The verse recalls the battle at Mount Carmel recorded in First Kings 18. In one corner is God's prophet, Elijah. In the other corner are the four hundred prophets of Baal, supported by Queen Jezebel. Both sides build altars, prepare bulls for sacrifice, and pile wood into pyres. Elijah goes a step further, soaking his wood with gallons of water. Then each prays for the fire to be lit from above, having agreed beforehand that "the god who answers by fire is indeed God."

Twice Elijah prays: "Let it be known this day that you are God…" When the fire from heaven consumes Elijah's offering, the people respond "The LORD indeed is God; the LORD indeed is God." Everyone knows who is God and who is not after such a decisive victory. The story ends with Elijah killing the prophets of Baal.

While the story makes for good theater, it offends modern sensibilities. What kind of God condones such a massacre? With respect to the warning to Thyatira, what kind of God slaughters children?

In the narrative genre of the Elijah story, as well as in the apocalyptic genre of Revelation, such language functions to force a decision. The language is neither a call to a bloody crusade nor a justification for holy wars against heretics. Rather, John employs a literary technique to encourage self-examination. The repentance he seeks is from the false prophet, her followers, and those who are tolerating them.

So, what was the false prophet teaching? Without explanation, the letter simply refers to "what some call 'the deep things of Satan.'" But what could those teachings be?

Hard to imagine is that the explicit teaching of satanic worship would be tolerated in any church even for a micro-second. So that can't be it.

One theory tortuously argues that Jezebel was teaching that "the really wise and mature Christian must know life at its worst as well as at its best…[and therefore it is] right and necessary to commit the grossest and the most depraved sins, in order to experience what they were like."[45] But is it conceivable that a church praised for its "love, faith, service, and patient endurance," whose "last works are greater than the first," would tolerate such an extreme?

---

[45] Barclay. Page 78.

Some suggest the "deep things" consisted of some secret knowledge necessary for salvation, perhaps a form of Gnosticism. If so, then the reference to the "deep things of Satan" rather than to the "deep things of God" must be sarcastic.

The truth is no one knows what she was teaching. What we do know is that she was no messenger from God and her teachings were not of God, no matter how earnestly she proclaimed them.

But what about the rest of the church, those who have not been tolerating her and her teachings? Proclaims the Risen Christ: "I do not lay on you any other burden; only hold fast to what you have until I come."

It sounds a bit like they are getting off easy. But the answer begs another question: "any other burden" than what? The church already is bearing the yoke of discipleship through its "love," "faith," "service," and "patient endurance." It already is engaged in doing "greater works" than before. Now it needs to silence the false prophet and say "no" to her teachings. Its new burden is to return to its previous healthy behavior as a church by avoiding the conflict no longer and dealing directly with the problem at hand.

"To everyone who conquers and continues to do my works to the end," the Risen Christ promises, "I will give authority over the nations; to rule them with an iron rod, as when clay pots are shattered – even as I also received authority from my father."

This promise comes directly from Psalm 2, one of the royal psalms, perhaps originally used in a coronation. The psalmist sings of God's anointed son assuming the throne of David, where he exercises authority over nations and sovereigns. Power is in his hands.

In choosing this particular psalm, John returns to the "Son of God" image with which he begins. He promises a city with no natural defenses, which perhaps never won a battle in its history, overrun by empire after empire after empire, that the tables will be turned in God's realm. He promises a church made up of common laborers a shared place on God's throne.

And then he makes the best promise of all: "To the one who conquers I will give the morning star." Generally, the "morning star" is understood as "...the dawn of a new day, and the fulfillment of hope after the night of longing..."[46] More specifically, the "morning star" is associated with Venus, the god to whom Roman generals built temples, whose symbol was placed on the standards of the Roman legions. Promised to this church is the presence of the one who is victorious in the ultimate battle with evil itself. As it is written in Revelation 22:16...

---

[46]Metzger. Page 37.

It is I, Jesus, who sent my angel to you with this testimony for the churches. I am the root and the descendant of David. I am the bright morning star.

Let anyone who has an ear listen
to what the Spirit is saying
to the churches.

7 SARDIS

Lest he slip on the snow covered steps, Harold climbs slowly, cane in right hand, left on the railing. He hangs his coat on a hanger salvaged from the rummage sale, still covered with the dry cleaner's ad. Entering the sanctuary he rests for a moment in the third pew from the back on the pulpit side that his family has occupied every Sunday morning for the last four generations.

Since Mildred passed away three years ago, he has been alone in that pew. Their children left the farm long before, first off to college, then married, finding employment in other cities. Following World War II the church filled with young families. Now on a good Sunday there are thirty gray-hairs like himself. The rays of the setting sun through the stain-glass window lands just before the altar, where Mildred's casket rested for the funeral.

Harold picks up their hymnal from the rack, the one Mildred and he purchased for the church, with their nameplate in the front. The next to the last pastor pressured the congregation into purchasing new hymnals which left out old favorites and changed familiar words. Upon her leaving they went back in their boxes and the old beloved ones reappeared. The last pastor tried convincing the church that they didn't need hymnbooks at all, just a multimedia projector and a screen. That was the end of him.

Before moving on to the search committee meeting in the parlor, Harold pauses at the front of the sanctuary to look once more at the hanging Mildred and the other women quilted for the last anniversary celebration:

Fifth Church
1849 to 1999
150 Years of Service

The year is 2011.

3:1 *Write to the angel of the church in Sardis! Thus saith the one holding the seven spirits of God and the seven stars. I know your accomplishments: that you have a reputation that you are alive, but you are dead.*

2 *Wake up! Strengthen now what is at death's door! For, in the judgment of my God, I have not found your works to have been completed.*

3 *Remember, therefore, in what manner you have received and heard! Keep guard! Repent! If you do not stay alert, then I may come like a thief and you will not know which hour I shall come upon you.*

4 *Nevertheless you have a few persons in Sardis who dirtied not their garments, and, because they are worthy, they will parade with me in white.*

5 *The victor, in this way, will clothe him/herself in white garments. Not only will I not erase his/her name from the book of life, I also will confess his/her name before my father and before his angels.*

6 *Whoever has an ear, hear what the spirit is saying to the churches!*

Sardis is in wine country. Vineyards cover hills and valleys. Perhaps that is why the ancients believed it was the birthplace of Dionysus – the Greek god credited with teaching the secrets to cultivating vines and fermenting grapes.

 The myth claims Dionysus' divine father was Zeus and his human mother was Semele. Supposedly Zeus took Dionysus out of Semele's womb and carried him to term in his thigh. Accordingly, Dionysus was said to be twice born. One story claims Dionysus changed water into wine. Because two of his festivals were connected with the onset of winter and the greening of spring, associated with his name was the promise of resurrection.

The last god to enter the Olympian panoply, Dionysus was different. With ritual sacrifices marked by order, Greek religion tended to appeal to rationality. The followers of Dionysus, however, preferred mystery. Their worship emphasized intoxication. Alcohol was not necessarily involved. Rather, this cult sought the spiritual high, the ecstasy, the transformation experienced in festive celebrations, rapturous singing, and animated dancing – such activities being their means to connect with Dionysus in the hope of receiving the blessing of happiness which overcomes the sadness of this world.

To outsiders the high-spiritedness, infectious liveliness, and exuberant freedom of Dionysus' devotees appeared to be sheer madness, delusional ravings, or obscene revelry. But those inside the cult believed surrendering to the power of Dionysus, even though it meant abandoning cultural restrictions, increased their relationship with the spiritual.

At its worse, excessive celebration by the cult of Dionysus earned a reputation for drunkenness, frenzied dismembering of sacrificial animals with an accompanying eating of their bodies raw and drinking of their blood warm, and orgies. Reacting to reports of such extreme behaviors, in 186 BCE the Roman Senate banned the festival of *Bacchanalia* (Bacchus being the Roman name for the Greek god Dionysus). The law's intent was to hamper or halt the rumored practice; but it did not curtail this god's popularity in the first century CE.

At its best, the free expression felt and displayed by members of the cult was associated with creativity and the stage. The yearly rite celebrating the resurrection of Dionysus, with its masks and chorus, became the basic structure for Greek drama. Ancient competitions named after this god drew entries from such playwrights as Aeschylus, Sophocles, and Euripides. Temples to Dionysus were found wherever there were theaters in the Greco-Roman world. Libations at his altar preceded every performance.

While there are many stories about Dionysus, the most famous is King Midas – the tale of a mythical ruler of Phrygia who turns everything he touches into gold. In the story the one who gives Midas the golden touch is Dionysus, who warns the king his wealth will not bring happiness. When Midas finally learns that truth, he washes away his golden touch in the waters of the Pactolus River. That river runs through Sardis.

From 570 to 546 BCE, Sardis was ruled by a fabulously wealthy monarch, the legendary King Croesus. At that time Sardis was the capital of the Lydian empire which stretched from the Aegean Sea into what is now central Turkey. Sardis was the hub of five major roads. Harvard's Janet Tassel notes that according to the first century Greek historian of the Roman Empire, Dio Chrysostom: "the river Pactolus...swirled down from the heights of Mount Tmolus laden with gold dust, right 'through the middle of Sardis,' bringing unimaginable riches to Croesus just 'for the taking.'"[47]

Was there gold in the Pactolus River? Or did its golden sand become a symbol for a fortune built from agriculture and commerce? Most likely "both" is the right answer. Archeologists confirm the existence of a gold

---

[47] Tassel, Janet. "The Search for Sardis." *Harvard Magazine*. March 1998. Downloaded from http://www.harvardmag.com/ma98/sardis.html.

refinery in Sardis. Wine-making continues as a significant industry in the region. Add the number of major roads running through the city and all the elements are there for the creation of capital.

Sardis minted the world's first coins during the reign of King Croesus – gold and silver pieces recognized and accepted without weighing, backed by the full faith and confidence of the vast wealth in Croesus' treasury.

Herodotus (the fifth century BCE Greek historian) tells the story of King Croesus, the richest person in the world, inviting Solon, the wisest person on the face of the earth, to see his storerooms filled with gold. Tour complete, Croesus asks Solon: "Who is the happiest person in the universe?" Croesus expects Solon to acknowledge that he, the king, surely must be the happiest. Instead Solon names Tellus of Athens, whoever that is, and proceeds to give the king a lecture on how once a person has enough to meet his or her daily needs, happiness comes not with how much money one accumulates but in how one lives her or his life.

Cyrus the Persian ultimately conquers King Croesus and the Lydians. As Herodotus tells the story, a pyre is lit to burn Croesus at the stake. Cyrus – hearing the king call out "Solon! Solon! Solon!" – orders the flames doused and asks Croesus what Solon told him. Croesus counters with a question of his own: "What are your soldiers doing right now?" "They are plundering *your* city and carrying off *your* treasures," Cyrus replies. "But nothing belongs to me anymore," Croesus retorts; "now *you* are the one they are robbing."

The god of wine? The god of wealth? Are either or both of these gods the Risen Christ's primary concern with the church in Sardis?

Some commentators jump to the conclusion that the extremes associated with these two gods – namely licentiousness and luxurious living – surely must have characterized the people of this city. What else would so anger the Risen Christ that he could not offer, as in the other six letters, a single word of praise?

To be sure John shows no reluctance in condemning such behavior in Revelation. However, no explicit reference to the cult, drunkenness, sexual immortality, or the rich and famous can be found in the letter to Sardis itself.

The historical fact is that Sardis was no longer wealthy at the time of Revelation's writing, its glory days over for centuries. Ephesus was the "Supreme Metropolis of Asia." Smyrna was the "Most Beautiful City of Asia." Pergamum was the "Capital City of Asia." When the earthquakes hit in 17 CE, Laodicea rebuilt without any assistance from Rome; Philadelphia was thankful the Romans suspended taxes for five years so they could divert resources to rebuilding; but once unimaginably wealthy Sardis was so poor that Emperor Tiberius not only suspended taxation, he also awarded an incredibly large grant of ten million sesterces.

Moreover, no historical evidence indicates that the worst excesses of the cult of Dionysus, outlawed by Rome three hundred years earlier, reappeared in Sardis, if they were ever practiced there. "The Party Town of Asia" was never Sardis' claim to fame.

Other commentators conclude the sin of the church in Sardis was acculturation. They argue that given an opportunity to witness to their faith in the public square, the Christians in Sardis chose to go along with the crowd, striving not to change society but to assimilate. However, this misinterpretation is based on an erroneous dating of the ruins.

Sardis is not a popular destination today. On our last visit we had the entire site to ourselves, save for a guard at the ticket booth and one other family. While the ruins are not as expansive as Ephesus or Pergamum, they are spectacular.

Driving through the valley along the front of the mountain range, identifying Mount Tmolus is easy. Three sides of the mountain rise perpendicular to the valley below, with only a narrow ridge on the fourth side for access. No wonder King Croesus thought he was safe and his treasure secure, high on an impregnable peak. A remnant of the citadel's wall on the ridge still can be seen from the road.

Entry into the lower city at the mountain's base is by walking along an ancient street flanked by Roman columns on one side and the ruins of shops on the other. Thirty-three adjoining businesses, abutting the outside wall of a Roman gymnasium, form the business district. Sheep and goat bones suggest at least one of the stores served as a restaurant. Found in the ruins of the rest were coins, dyes, glass, jewelry, metal utensils, pottery, and tools.

Chiseled menorahs and crosses suggest Christians and Jews worked side-by-side in Sardis. But, contrary to what some argue, these symbols do not prove a few in Sardis mustered the courage to witness to the faith at the time of Revelation's writing. While the Roman columns stood during John's day, the shops date no earlier than the fourth century CE.

Behind the Byzantine shops is a partially reconstructed imperial-style Roman gymnasium-bath-court complex. Roman gymnasiums were for training the body and the mind. Roman baths were for physical therapy and mental relaxation. This complex, covering nearly a quarter-million square feet, was the center of Sardis' community life.

Sharing a wall with the Roman gymnasium are the ruins of the largest synagogue unearthed from antiquity. Three hundred ninety-four feet long by fifty-nine feet wide, its sanctuary accommodated a thousand worshippers. Entry is from the east through a courtyard with fountain. On the back wall are two niches which housed the Torah scrolls. In the front is an apse with three curved rows to seat the synagogue's elders. The floors are mosaic and the walls inlaid marble. A stone table sits centered before the apse, with an eagle carved on the outside of each twin slab supporting the table's top. Parallel to the table and a few feet to either side are a pair of lion statues.

Approximately eighty inscriptions were discovered in the synagogue during excavations in the 1960s, six in Hebrew and the rest in Greek, the first to appear being the word *shalom*. These inscriptions include the names of various Jewish benefactors and their spouses, along with God-fearers (non-members whom today we might call "seekers"). Some bear titles of local governmental officials. Others list their vocation as goldsmiths. One is identified as a priest and teacher of wisdom.

Some teach that the Jewish population in Sardis dates to the fall of Jerusalem in 586 BCE, to the Babylonian Exile, to the time of the Diaspora when the Jewish people were scattered to cities outside the Promised Land. Others trace its beginnings to an invitation to relocate in Sardis extended by the Seleucid King Antiochus III (223-187 BCE).

The proximity of the synagogue to the Roman gymnasium-bath-court complex rather than to the Jewish residential quarter, together with the presence in the sanctuary of eagles (typically emblematic of Rome) and lions (a common symbol for the goddess Cybele), have led some to deduce that the Jewish people of Sardis broke their covenant with God to remain distinctive, becoming indistinguishable from the city's general population.

Elsewhere on the site, a church building attached to the ruins of a temple assumed to have been dedicated to Cybele appears to suggest Christians living in Sardis committed the same sin.

But is that the case? If so, why does the Risen Christ not rail against the unfaithfulness of this significant synagogue in Sardis as he does in the letters to Smyrna and Philadelphia? And in which verse does John write a single word suggesting the Christians in Sardis needed to confront their allegiance to the god of societal capitulation?

Morever, the construction of the Christian church is Byzantine. Built no earlier than the fifth century CE, no Christians worshipped there when John wrote Revelation. Nor at that time did anyone worship Cybele on that site.

Cybele was the local name for Kubaba – the ancient Anatolian mother goddess. In 498 BCE the Athenian army destroyed the temple to Cybele built by King Croesus near the Pactolus River to protect his gold. On the grounds where that temple once stood, a century and a half later, in 334 BCE, Alexander the Great erected a temple to Artemis (the Greek goddess most resembling Kubaba/Cybele). While the evolution of the goddess from Kubaba to Cybele to Artemis may seem a distinction without a difference, no one should ignore the hard historical fact that the ruins of the temple by the Byzantine church have laid on the ground since 17 CE. No one rebuilt the temple after the earthquake. So no one worshipped anyone or anything at that site when Revelation was written.

Moreover, the synagogue could not have existed next to the Roman gymnasium-bath-court complex when John wrote, since the complex was not yet built! Dedicated to Julia Domna, wife of Emperor Septimius Severus, it was not finished until 212 CE. Once erected, the Roman complex included three rooms apparently designed for resting and dressing. In time those three rooms were converted into one very long room to serve as a public meeting place or civic center. That space then was transformed into the Jewish synagogue sometime between the fourth and the sixth centuries CE, based upon coins found beneath the mosaic floor.

Furthermore, an alternative explanation to assimilation exists for the sanctuary's eagles and lions. According to Tel Aviv University's Nahum Goldmann Museum of the Jewish Diaspora: "…both animals expressed also a strong Jewish symbolism, especially the lion, a common motif of Jewish art of the epoch that had long been emblematically associated with the Tribe of Judah and the city of Jerusalem."[48]

A danger in scriptural interpretation is engaging in eisogesis rather than exegesis – reading into a passage one's personal beliefs rather than reading out of the text the author's message. Similarly, one must not construe what the archaeological ruins do not substantiate.

A prophetic word comes from the Risen Christ who has "the seven spirits of God and the seven stars." As previously explained in the chapter on Ephesus, we know from Revelation 1 that the seven stars is a symbol for the angels of the seven churches. Also mentioned in that first chapter of Revelation are the "seven spirits who are before God's throne." Perhaps these are angelic beings. Perhaps the phrase refers to the Holy Spirit. But consistent with the theology of Revelation's author is that they symbolize attributes of God found in the Risen Christ.

Isaiah 9 is familiar, often read during Advent, and understood from the earliest days of the Christianity to be about Jesus the Messiah:

> A shoot shall come out from the stump of Jesse,
>   and a branch shall grow out of his roots.
> The spirit of the Lord shall rest on him.
>   The spirit of wisdom and understanding.
>   The spirit of counsel and might.
>   The spirit of knowledge and the fear of the Lord.
> His delight shall be in the fear of the Lord.

Note only six spirits are listed: (1) wisdom, (2) understanding, (3) counsel, (4) might, (5) knowledge, and (6) awe. Remember Sardis was a Hellenistic city

---

[48] Downloaded October 16, 2006. http://www.bh.org.il/communities/Synagogue/Sardis.asp.

in which Greek was the spoken language. Christians there read the Septuagint – the Greek translation of Hebrew scripture – which adds a seventh: "the spirit of piety."

"I know your works…" the Risen Christ continues. The congregation in Sardis just heard read the letters to the first four churches. In each the Risen Christ said "I know you works…" followed by a word of praise. Praise for the Ephesians' toil, endurance, and testing of false prophets. Praise for the Smyrnians' perseverance in the face of affliction, poverty, and slander. Praise for the Pergamenes' holding fast to the name of Christ. Praise for the Thyatirians' love, faith, service, endurance, and ever greater and greater good works. Were the Sardians about to be praised for displaying the attributes of the seven spirits?

But no compliment follows. None. Theirs is the only church not praised for anything. "I know your works: you have a name of being alive, but you are dead."

Dead. Not dead as in Paul's theology where he speaks of "dying in Christ in order to be raised with Christ." No, dead as in corpses. Dead as in graves. Dead as in tumuli – those huge Lydian burial mounds in the fields outside the city. Dead as in no longer breathing. Dead as in no longer having the *ruah* – the breath of God – within them. Dead as in having no spirit at all.

The residents of Sardis have a name. They have a reputation. There are lots of stories about them. But all are in past tense.

Here is one recorded in the *Annals* of Tacitus (the first century CE Roman historian who chronicled the reigns from Augustus through Domitian). The setting is the decision in 26 CE to authorize the building of a temple to Emperor Tiberias and his mother Livia, somewhere in the province of Asia. Eleven cities bid for the honor of hosting the imperial cult. Nine applications are considered and rejected quickly, either because a similar temple already exists or because the cities are too poor to afford one. The last two contenders are Smyrna and Sardis. Appearing before a tribunal of the Roman Senate, the equivalent of the Sardis Chamber of Commerce makes a case on the basis of their city's glorious history. The delegation from Smyrna speaks of their city's promising future. Smyrna is selected over Sardis.

Is it not fascinating that the Risen Christ speaks to Smyrna in precisely the opposite way that he speaks to Sardis? In the letter to Smyrna the movement is from death to life. In the letter to Sardis, it is from life to death.

The church in Sardis is Christian in name only. It isn't that it is on automatic pilot, in cruise control, or propelled by inertia. It is worse. It is resting on its laurels, sleeping on the job, following perhaps the most common false god plaguing the Christian movement to this day. The church is worshipping the god of its past.

"Wake up!" John writes in the first of five imperative instructions shouted by the Risen Christ with punctuated intensity. If he didn't have their attention before, he certainly does with the choice of those two words.

Here is another story from Sardis' past. In 549 BCE the armies of Cyrus the Persian mounted camels and attacked the horse-riding cavalry of King Croesus. Herodotus writes that because horses cannot stand to be in the presence of camels, Croesus' forces turned and galloped up the ridge to the citadel for safety. Cyrus' troops stayed below, laying siege, waiting. After two weeks Cyrus became impatient and offered a reward to anyone finding a way to storm the sheer cliffs. A Persian soldier named Hyeroeades was standing watch when a Lydian fighter dropped his helmet, picked his way down the rock face to get it, and scrambled back up. That night a Persian strike force climbed stealthily by that same route. Sound asleep, the garrisons on top never dreamed anyone could reach them in their "impregnable" fortress.

While it may sound unbelievable, history repeated itself in 218 BCE. The Seleucid armies of Antiochus III similarly attacked the precipice at night, breaching the unguarded fortress atop while Sardis' military personnel snored in their barracks.

"Wake up!" shouts the Risen Christ. The verb is in the present imperative, meaning wake up and stay awake.

"Strengthen what remains and is on the point of death!" – an aorist imperative verb implying they can't continue as they have any longer. They must get up and get going, not later but now.

Then another present imperative: "Remember" – and bear in mind – "what you received and heard!" They know what they are to do.

Then a third present imperative: "Obey it!" No more glorying in the past. No more resting on laurels. No more stepping aside hoping someone else will carry the load. God expects the church to do God's will – and keep on doing it – for as long as there is any life in it.

Why? The Risen Christ explains: "For I have not found your works perfect (better translated "completed") in the sight of my God."

Finally, "Repent!" Another aorist imperative indicating they must decide then and there to turn their lives around one hundred eighty degrees. Living in the past is not acceptable, not when the Risen Christ calls the church to engage fully in the battle against evil now.

Then the warning: "I will come like a thief, and you will not know at what hour I will come." Some believe this an allusion to the second coming. Metaphorical use of such language in connection with the return of Christ is found in Paul's epistles, Peter's writings, as well as in the apocalyptic discourses of the first three gospels. However, it is conspicuously absent in the Gospel According to John, as well as in the First, Second, and Third Letters of John. Far more likely is that John is using Sardis' past against it to underscore his point. These words re-emphasize the previous imperatives.

The residents of Sardis remember how the city slept when Cyrus came. They remember how it slumbered when Antiochus arrived. Now they must not forget that the Risen Christ does not want to catch them napping again.

"Yet you have still a few persons in Sardis who have not soiled their clothes," the letter continues.

Some try reading this verse as a veiled reference either to the blood the revelers of the Dionysus cult inadvertently splattered on their clothes as they allegedly ripped the sacrificial animals apart with their bare hands during the festival of *Bacchanalia,* or else to the blood of sacrificial animals cascading down upon the worshippers of Cybele waiting in a pit below the altar. Neither interpretation is compelling given the lack of any evidence that such activities were occurring at the time of Revelation's writing, if they ever occurred in Sardis' history.

Others try tying this verse to inscriptions archaeologists discovered in various temples throughout the province of Asia warning worshipers that because dirty clothes are an affront to the gods, proper attire is required to enter the sanctuary – the ancient equivalent of parents insisting children put on their Sunday best before going to church. However, if the allusion to blood seems too much, a connection to mere dust feels too little.

More in keeping with the theology and style of John is a passage of Hebrew scripture seldom read in the modern church – a story found in the third chapter of Zechariah.

About thirty years after Cyrus captured the sleeping city of Sardis, Zechariah received a series of night visions. In the fourth night vision he sees the high priest Joshua standing before the angel of the Lord. Joshua wears dirty clothes. Satan is bringing charges against him.

At this point in history, the word "Satan" was not understood as a personal name for the prince of evil. Rather, the word meant "accuser." It was a technical term for the prosecuting attorney in the heavenly courtroom.

In Zechariah's night vision the angel orders Joshua's dirty clothes removed. "Take off his filthy clothes!" the angel commands. Then he says to Joshua, "See, I have taken your guilt away from you, and I will clothe you with festal apparel." Next the angel delivers a "Thus saith the Lord" message from God to Joshua. Joshua is expected to "walk in [God's] ways and to keep [God's] requirements." The fourth night vision ends with Zechariah hearing this word from God: "I will remove the guilt of this land in a single day…and you shall invite each other to come under your vine and fig tree." Throughout Hebrew scripture references to people sitting under their vine and their fig tree point toward the future blessings of the Promised Land.

John knows the prophecy of Zechariah. So do the members of the church in Sardis. When they hear Revelation's references to "dirty clothes," "walking with," and "white robes," they made a connection most today would not think to make.

"They will walk with me dressed in white, for they are worthy," the Risen Christ promises. "If you conquer, you will be clothed like them in white robes." White: the color of triumph. White: the color of celebrations. White: the color of guilt removed.

"I will not blot your name out of the book of life," the Risen Christ pledges. The idea that God has a divine registry in which the names of God's people are listed was common at the time of Revelation's writing. Interesting here, given the letter's preceding content, is that the vow is not that the Risen Christ will write people's names in the book of life if they get themselves out of bed and go to work, but rather that their names will not be erased. Such language reflects the usual practice in the Roman world of officials removing from the city's rolls the names of those who have died or have committed treasonous acts.

It also recalls the story of Moses and the golden calf, where the first prophet confesses to God that the people have worshipped another god. Moses pleads for their forgiveness lest God "blot out of [God's] book" their names. The good news here is that despite the deadness of the church in Sardis, there still is hope, the hope of resurrected life, both in this world and in the world to come.

The Risen Christ then makes another covenant: "I will confess your name before my father and before his angels." His oath is the opposite side of the coin from the ominous notice Jesus gave during his earthly ministry when he said: "Those who are ashamed of me and of my words in this adulterous and sinful generation, of them the Son of Man also will be ashamed when he comes in the glory of his father with the holy angels."

The twentieth century British theologian, William Barclay, captures the essence of the message to Sardis when he writes: "A church is in danger of death when it begins to worship its own past, when it lives on its memories instead of finding a challenge in its hopes, when it is more taken up with its traditions than its ideals."[49]

Let anyone who has an ear listen
to what the Spirit is saying
to the churches.

---

[49] Barclay, Page 87.

8 PHILADELPHIA

Sixth Church knows what is expected. Its mission is implanted in its genetic code, penned in its charter, pounded into its conscience.

Birthed when the big church downtown commissioned a few families to start a satellite congregation on the city's growing edge, Sixth Church is to model itself after its parent, recreate the established church's style and program in the new location, and grow large enough to seed another church start.

But life in a small struggling church proved different than life in an affluent corporate-sized one. Somehow they thought if they opened their door, put "Everyone Welcome" on their sign, bold printed their name in the yellow pages, took out an ad in the newspaper, and called the right pastor, folk would flock to this wonderful opportunity to join the new congregation.

It did not happen. It does not look like it is going to happen any time soon. When the hurricane hit, flooding their sanctuary and tearing apart their social hall, the congregation feared it was all over.

Fortunately the big church downtown had kept Sixth Church's insurance premiums paid. Eventually the contractors restored the facilities to original condition: new chairs, spotless carpet, fresh paint – an opportunity to start over. But their hearts are not in it. The guest preacher at the re-dedication service thinks she knows what is wrong.

"How many of you, if you saw a great movie, would tell a friend about it?" she begins her charge. After an initial hesitancy most every hand goes up. "How many of you, if you read a good book, would loan it to a neighbor?" About the same number of hands. "If you were entertaining guests at a dinner party and someone asked for the secret family recipe, how many of you would share it?" Not nearly as many hands this time. Looking over the congregation she asks one last question: "How many of you invited someone to come with you to church this morning?"[50]

3:7 *Write to the angel of the church in Philadelphia! Thus saith the holy one, the true one, the one holding the key of David, the one who opens and no one will shut, and who shuts and no one opens.*

[8] I know your accomplishments. Listen! Since you possess insignificant resources, I have put before you a door that has been opened, which no one is capable of shutting. You kept my word. You renounced not my name.

[9] Listen! I will inflict punishment upon the synagogue of the adversary, those claiming to be themselves Jews, only they are not. They are but deceiving themselves. Listen! I will execute judgment upon them, so that they will appear and will bow down at your feet. They will learn that I love you.

[10] Since you kept my word of endurance, I will keep you from the hour of trial – the one intended to come upon the whole world – to try those living upon the earth.

[11] I am coming soon. Grab hold to what you have, so no one can take your crown!

[12] The victor, I will consider him/her a pillar in the temple of my God. Moreover, she/he need never leave there. I will write upon him/her the name of my God, the name of the city of my God (the New Jerusalem descending from the heavens of my God), and my new name.

[13] Whoever has an ear hear what the spirit is saying to the churches!

---

[50] Though not quoted precisely, the illustration originated in a charge given by the Rev. Jim Dewey, former Associate Conference Minister of the Indiana-Kentucky Conference of the United Church of Christ.

Philadelphia is the youngest of the seven cities. Most scholars credit King Attalus II of Pergamum with founding "The City of Brotherly Love" in 140 BCE, though a few think its birth was a bit earlier during the reign of Eumenes II. The city's name reflects the closeness of the sibling sovereigns. While one followed the other on Pergamum's throne, Philadelphian coins bear both images together, as if Attalus and Eumenes were identical twins.

Pergamum was the capital, "The First City of Asia," a municipal masterpiece, the very best in Hellenistic culture. As discussed earlier, it was home to magnificent architecture, awesome sculptures, a premier library, an advanced medical complex, impressive temples, and altars to the greatest gods and goddesses in the Olympian panoply. The intent of the Pergemene kings was to make their city greater than Athens.

They were as purposeful in selecting the site for Philadelphia at the foot of, and on the road leading up to, the interior of the Anatolian plain. Their goal was to construct an outpost at the edge of their territory from which Hellenistic religion, customs, and thought could be shared with the barbarians to the east. (The word "barbarian" did not carry the pejorative sense it does today, but rather was a neutral term for people speaking a language other than Greek.) Philadelphia's mission was evangelistic: to spread the virtues of Hellenistic ways on the frontier.

While Philadelphia's location appears ideal for such a labor, there is no evidence the city enjoyed any success in accomplishing its mission, or that its citizens even tried. Why? Most likely because earthquakes diverted their energy.

Pergamum built Philadelphia at the edge of a region called the *katakekaumene* (the "burnt land"), where volcanic eruptions coupled with significant erosion to create strange rock formations, foul-smelling mineral-filled hot springs bubbling to the surface, and frequent sizeable seismic tremors, causing the fearful to tremble. "A city full of earthquakes" was the first century CE Greek geographer Strabo's summary description of the city.

One particularly devastating earthquake struck in 17 CE. Foundations crumbled. Ashlars tumbled. Buildings collapsed. That earthquake was to Philadelphia what the 1906 earthquake was to San Francisco. The destruction so extensive, the experience so traumatic, Strabo reports three years later many still lived in huts outside the city rather than risk being struck by falling or flying debris from cracked buildings kept standing by makeshift supports.

News of this natural disaster traveled far. Emperor Tiberius suspended taxation for five years and provided substantial relief funds so that the Philadelphians could rebuild. So thankful were the citizens that they renamed their city *Neocaesarea* ("The New City of Caesar").

Half a century later they changed their name again to "Flavia" – the family name of Emperor Vespasian.

Today a very small beautifully kept garden encloses the few remaining archaeological fragments. A broken sarcophagus and other minor artifacts lie next to a path beside the ruins of a basilica with traces of an eleventh century fresco made faint by centuries of exposure to the elements. What impresses is the sheer thickness of the Byzantine brick pillars. Pillars built to last through an earthquake. Pillars built to calm a people's fears.

Additionally, Philadelphia was situated on the eastern edge of a valley stretching west to the Aegean Sea at Smyrna, with perfect soil and climatic conditions for vineyards. Famed for the wine it produced, Philadelphia's economy was dependent upon grapes.

However, at the time of Revelation's writing, their economy was depressed severely due to a decree of Domitian. No, not the "Caesar is Lord" decree so offensive to John; but rather an imperial edict issued in 92 CE demanding that at least half of their vines be ripped out and no new ones planted. Perhaps Domitian wanted to encourage the production of grain instead. More likely he wanted to protect the economic interests of the wine industry nearer to Rome. Whatever the case, the negative economic impact of that unpopular decision was another unnerving disaster, made worse when a major famine broke out leaving Philadelphia with neither food nor sufficient profits from their grapes to buy food.[51]

"These are the words of the holy one, the true one, who has the key of David, who opens and no one will shut, who shuts and no one opens." Unlike the first five letters, these titles are not found in the first chapter of Revelation. Even the reference to a key is different, here being "the key of David" rather than Revelation 1's "keys of Death and Hades."

With one exception, the word "holy" is not used in Hebrew scripture to describe any individual. Certain places where God is found are recognized as holy: Jerusalem, the Temple, the Holy of Holies, the hills, the mountains, the habitation of the Most High. Items related to the worship of God are called holy: altars and offerings, incense and oil, festival days and the Sabbath. The covenants God makes with the people, as well as the people's promises to God, are considered holy. The priests and the Levites as groups are deemed holy, not because of any personal righteousness but in relation to being set apart to minister in God's name. Chosen by God for a purpose, God's people as a whole are called to be and to behave as a holy nation. Of course God's Spirit is holy, as are the spiritual beings surrounding God's holy throne.

But the only time the word "holy" is applied to a specific human being is in Second Kings 4:8-10 where a wealthy woman tries to convince her husband to build an extra room on their house for the prophet Elisha (who

---

[51] Worth. *...Roman Culture.* Page 67.

eats with them whenever he passes through town), because she is sure he is "a holy man of God."

That vignette is the exception to the rule. Only God is holy in Hebrew scripture. God alone is the Holy One. The holiness of anything else derives from God being holy. "Holy, holy, holy is the Lord of hosts," Isaiah hears the seraphim singing, "the whole earth is full of God's glory!"

In Revelation, John, too, hears creatures around God's throne singing "Holy, holy, holy, the Lord God the Almighty, who was and is and is to come." Moreover, in the fourth and fifth chapters of Revelation, the heavenly court praises both God and the Lamb as "worthy to receive glory and honor and power." In referring to the Risen Christ as "the holy one," the letter to Philadelphia makes an extraordinary theological claim: it specifically equates Jesus with God.

"These are the words of the holy, the true one..." Another word seldom if ever applied in the scriptures to a person is the word "true." The Greek is *alethinos*, which carries the sense of being authentic, the genuine article, the real thing.

The third title – "who has the key of David, who opens and no one will shut, who shuts and no one opens" – essentially is a quote from Isaiah 22:22. The reason that particular verse was especially poignant to the Philadelphians is missed unless one recognizes the parallel between the disheartenment they felt living in a disaster-prone area and the discouragement expressed by the inhabitants of Jerusalem prior to the fall of that city.

Isaiah knows Jerusalem is going to be destroyed. Shoring up the city's defenses will not stop God's judgment upon the people's unfaithfulness. Tearing down their homes to fortify the city will be in vain. The walls are going to be battered down no matter what they do. Recognizing the utter futility of their efforts, the Jerusalemites take on an "eat and drink for tomorrow we may die" air of hopelessness.

But Isaiah tells them there is reason to hope nevertheless. The impending decimation of their city, however traumatic, will not mean their ultimate demise. God still has more in store for them. God is granting authority over God's people to God's faithful servant, Eliakim. "I will place on his shoulder the key of the house of David; he shall open and no one will shut; he shall shut and no one shall open."

Surely the Philadelphians heard those three titles as reassurance in their shattered world. Founded by secular authorities intent on having their philosophy of life spread beyond their borders, now they are being addressed by God regarding God's mission for them. Economically decimated by Domitian's edict in 92 CE, which revealed the emperor's indifference to their welfare, now comes a message from the God who cares about their needs. Having been shaken to their foundations by earthquakes destroying their city again and again, now they are listening to the steadfastly faithful one in whom they legitimately can place their trust, because authority over their lives belongs to the Risen Christ.

"I know your works. Look, I have set before you an open door, which no one is able to shut." Some interpret this verse as God offering the Philadelphian church members lives of endless possibilities. Others suggest "open door" refers to prayer as the doorway to God, to Jesus as the door to salvation, or to some door leading into heaven's glory. Such misinterpretations fail to recognize the phrase "open door" as first century technical language for an evangelistic charge – a point not missed in a city founded with a missionary purpose. Consider these passages regarding Paul's calling and work:

> When they arrived [in Antioch], they called the church together and related all that God had done with them, and how God had opened a door of faith for the Gentiles. (Acts 14:27)

> But I will stay in Ephesus until Pentecost, for a wide door for effective work has opened to me, and there are many adversaries. (I Corinthians 16:8-9)

> When I came to Troas to proclaim the good news of Christ, a door was opened for me in the Lord. (II Corinthians 2:12)

> At the same time pray for us as well that God will open to us a door for the word, that we may declare the mystery of Christ, for which I am in prison, so that I may reveal it clearly, as I should. (Colossians 4:3-4)

The church in the city founded as a missionary outpost for Hellenism now is chartered with a different mission. The battle between God and the gods is not simply defensive. It is not just a war of resistance. It involves actively engaging in sharing the faith with those who know only the gods and goddesses of the world, enlisting them to join the community of the church in the battle against evil, publicly proclaiming the good news of the one who is holy, genuine, and steadfastly faithful.

Furthermore, in direct contrast to the city's history of failure as missionaries of Hellenism, the church in Philadelphia is promised that no earthquake, emperor, or edict can shut the door on their evangelistic efforts.

Fascinatingly, the two churches to receive letters without criticism from the Risen Christ, the two churches which thought they were poor and powerless, Smyrna and Philadelphia, are the same two cities of Revelation which today enjoy significant Christian populations.

"I know that you have but little power, and yet you have kept my word and have not denied my name. I will make those of the synagogue of Satan who say that they are Jews and are not, but are lying – I will make them come and bow down before your feet, and they will learn that I have loved you."

Here is another scriptural passage readily subject to misinterpretation. Does the first sentence link to the previous verse so that we understand God is opening the door to the mission field and, because they remain faithful, is keeping it open for them despite their weakness? Or does it more naturally connect with what follows regarding the synagogue, helping to describe the local situation, thereby explaining away what otherwise appears to be anti-Semitic language? We believe the latter.

In the chapter on the letter to Smyrna, we noted John wrote when it was unclear if Christianity was a Jewish sect or a separate religion, when that question became even more divisive with the introduction of Gentile believers, and when the distancing of Christianity appeared to be in the best interest of Judaism given certain considerations provided by the Romans which could be removed should the government perceive Christianity a threat to the order. For example, in addition to being permitted to pray for the emperor instead of to the emperor, in 49 BCE the Jewish population in Asia was granted an exemption from being drafted into the Roman legions even during periods of emergency.[52]

John himself is a member of the Jewish faith who believes Jesus is the Messiah promised in Hebrew scripture. Given that reality, writes Bruce Metzger, "...we must not take the expression 'those of the synagogue of Satan' (3:9) in an anti-Jewish or anti-Semitic sense. The synagogue at Philadelphia was criticized, not for being Jewish, but for being hostile to Christians."[53] Metzger's argument is that a lack of hospitality by Jews shown to Jews who had accepted Jesus as the promised Messiah resulted in a judgment against this one particular synagogue – not in a condemnation of all Jewish people.

Understanding the intent of the last line in this section – "I will make them come and bow down before your feet, and they will learn that I have loved you" – requires our recognizing that John is returning to two additional passages from Isaiah.

The first phrase refers to a prophetic word to God's people upon returning to Jerusalem after the Babylonian captivity. Their city lies in ruins.

---

[52] Worth. ...*Roman Culture*. Page 25.

[53] Metzger. Page 41.

Before them is rebuilding. In a passage often read during the Epiphany season, Isaiah prophesies of a time when that work is completed:

> Arise, shine; for your light has come,
>   and the glory of the Lord has risen upon you…
> Nations shall come to your light,
>   and kings to the brightness of your dawn…
> The descendants of those who oppressed you
>   shall come bending low to you,
> And all who despised you
>   shall bow down at your feet;
> They shall call you the City of the Lord,
>   the Zion of the Holy One of Israel.

While initially it appears Isaiah 60 is about tables being turned, the oppressed becoming the powerful, and the persecuted held in adulation, closer inspection reveals it is not about vindication, punishment, or retribution. Rather, it is about God being recognized universally as God, God's will being followed by all, and God being worshipped by those who currently bow down before other gods and goddesses.

The Greek word translated "bow down" in the letter to Philadelphia is *proskuveo* which means "to fall down and worship," "to kneel before and venerate," "to fall at another's feet and do reverence." In the battle between God and the gods, the very last message John wants to send is that anyone or anything is worthy of being worshipped other than God and the Risen Christ…including the Philadelphian Christians!

John then alludes to another passage in Isaiah, this one from the time when the people of God were in captivity, so discouraged that they hung up their harps on the willow trees, unable to sing God's song in a foreign land. In that most demoralizing of moments, Isaiah 43:1-4a proclaims:

> Do not fear, for I have redeemed you;
>   I have called you by name, you are mine.
> When you pass through the waters, I will be with you…
>   When you walk through fire you shall not be burned…
> For I am the Lord your God, the Holy One of Israel, your Savior…
>   You are precious in my sight, and honored, and I love you.

In light of John's understanding of who is worthy of worship and who is not, along with his allusions to these two prophetic words from Isaiah, the line's intent becomes clearer. Given precarious living conditions in an earthquake-prone region, given the city's history of failure in missionary activity, given the demise of their economy caused by Emperor Domitian, given a poor relationship with the local synagogue, given their understandably low spirits, the Risen Christ assures them the day will come when the church's evangelistic mission will prove fruitful – when even those who excluded Christians from their love will be drawn to the love of God witnessed in God's love for them.

But that time is not yet.

"Because you have kept my word with patient endurance, I will keep you from the hour of trial that is coming on the whole world to test the inhabitants of the earth," the Risen Christ continues; "I am coming soon; hold fast to what you have, so that no one may seize your crown."

John is not Pollyannaish with respect to the church confronting the principalities and powers. Having stood at the foot of the cross, he had seen Jesus nailed upon it. He has outlived all the other disciples, every one of whom had met with a violent death. He knew Paul was thrown into jail for daring to evangelize on the frontier. He recognizes that the ostracizing of Philadelphian Christians from the synagogue is not going to end immediately.

Yes, John believes the return of Christ is imminent. But he also knows that it might not be today or tomorrow or even next week, next month, or next year.

So we believe it better to translate the preposition as "through" rather than "from," so that this verse reads "I will keep you through the hour of trial…" Certainly that would be consistent with the description of God supporting God's people through difficult times, as found in the Isaiah passage to which John refers.

The rest of the words in this verse, used in the previous five letters, are explained in previous chapters. "Patient endurance" does not connote passive acceptance but dogged determination and persistent resolve. "Hold fast" in the present imperative means to grab tightly and to keep a firm grip. The word for "crown" denotes not the royal diadem but the festal wreath.

"If you conquer," the Risen Christ concludes, "I will make you a pillar…"

"Do you know what 'a pillar of the church' is?" my mentor during my first year in parish ministry asked after a particularly difficult week. "No," I replied, sensing a joke coming. "Someone who is old and square and can't be moved!" he said.

The image of a pillar in this sixth letter in Revelation is intended to bring to mind something so strong, sound, steady, sturdy, solid, stable, and secure that it will stand even when everything around it is shaking.

Interestingly, the Risen Christ promises to make this church "…a pillar in the temple of my God…" The Greek word translated "temple" is *vaos* – the word naming the innermost sanctuary of the Jerusalem Temple, the court nearest to the Holy of Holies. "You will never go out of it," the Risen Christ promises this church prohibited from worshipping at the synagogue.

To this church in a city which changed names twice in the first century CE – to this church in a city where today, knocked over and scattered on the ground, are pillars chiseled with the names of gods, goddesses, governmental officials, and wealthy patrons – the Risen Christ promises to engrave on their pillar "the name of my God, and the name of the city of my God, the new Jerusalem that comes down from my God out of heaven, and my own new name."

Implicit in this trinity is that while the city may belong to the Roman Empire, the church belongs to God. The congregation may be located in Philadelphia, but it is part of another city where (John envisions in Revelation 21:2-4) "…the home of God is among mortals… God will wipe every tear from their eyes… Mourning and crying and pain will be no more…" And because the church bears nothing less than the name of the Risen Christ, their mission is clear: to proclaim in word and deed that name before which every knee should bow, to the end that all may hear the good news and believe.

> *Let anyone who has an ear listen*
> *to what the Spirit is saying*
> *to the churches.*

Capadocia (where they filmed StarWars)

beautiful land formation

89

9 LAODICEA

The members of Seventh Church are getting along just fine by themselves, thank you. With a beloved pastor, outstanding organist, full church school, active youth program, local mission projects, and healthy endowment, they are not looking for help from anyone.

Seventh Church does not participate in ecumenical projects or join in community worship celebrations. The pastor no longer attends clergy meetings. No delegates are present at regional church gatherings. Actions, issues, and concerns of the national church are not shared. No benevolent support goes to the international church. The bishop's office is never contacted. The denominational name has disappeared from stationary and signboard. Conversations continue about becoming an "independent church" (even if those two words do form an oxymoron).

When the envelopes arrive for the "Friends of the Wider Church" appeal – a yearly fund drive supporting ministry and mission beyond the doors of local churches – Seventh Church sent the cover-letter back with a scribbled note. It read: "We are no longer friends."

3:14 *Write to the angel of the church in Laodicea! Thus saith the amen, the trustworthy and true witness, the sovereign of God's creation.*

15 *I know your accomplishments: that you are neither cold nor hot. Would that you were cold or hot!*

[16] Under such circumstances, since you are lukewarm and neither hot nor cold, I am about to vomit you out of my mouth.

[17] You are saying: "I am wealthy and I have prospered and I have no need." You know not that you are wretched and pitiful and poor and blind and naked.

[18] I am advising you to purchase from me: gold that has been refined by fire, so that you might become rich; white garments, so that you yourself are clothed and the shame of your nakedness is not exposed; and eye salve to be rubbed on your eyes, so that you might see.

[19] As much as I love, I show fault and discipline. Therefore, be eager and repent!

[20] Listen! I have stood at the door and I am knocking. If anyone should hear my voice and open the door, I will come to him/her and I will dine with him/her, and he/she with me.

[21] The victor, I will permit her/him to sit with me on my throne that I won, even as I sat with my father on his throne.

[22] Whoever has an ear, hear what the spirit is saying to the churches!

A Laodicean villager waved down our rental car. "You're lost," he said; "You've driven past my house four times!" His smile conveyed nothing but a desire to help.

Hopping in the back seat, he navigated us a short distance down a country road. Passing the ancient aqueduct, he pointed across the railroad tracks to an unmarked opening in a fence. Just inside a carpet of grapes was drying into raisins. Obviously this was not the front gate. But we hadn't – and never would – find the official entrance. So we drove our benefactor home and returned to explore.

First we meandered through the weed-infested first century CE stadium, the postcard perfect ruins of the second century CE Roman bath and gymnasium, and the two theaters – one large, one small – opening toward a mile of spectacular white mineral deposits in the distance, cascading down the next mountain, forming a scenic backdrop for ancient stage productions.

Then, walking over the horizon, we happened upon archaeological finds not mentioned in any tour book, from the same general time period, only unearthed recently. There a guard spotted us, allowed one last picture on the colonnaded street, and escorted us toward the car.

The letter to Laodicea is the most famous of the seven. Parishioners vaguely remember somewhere in the scriptures is the image of Christ spewing a lukewarm church out of his mouth, along with a lingering childhood memory from red-lettered King James Bibles of Holman Hunt's portrait of Jesus standing outside the door knocking.

Yet, with its lack of hotels, restaurants, signage, and guides, tour buses by-pass Laodicea, destined instead for neighboring Pamukkale. The name means "Cotton Castle." There petrified calcareous terraces glisten in the sunlight, hot springs and wading pools invite playful relaxation, and the picturesque ruins of Hierapolis await. According to tradition, Philip introduced the gospel to that ancient city.

Laodicea's other neighbor, also left off travel itineraries, is Colossae, the recipient of a letter from Paul. The inter-relatedness of the tri-cities – Laodicea, Hierapolis, and Colossae – becomes apparent in Colossians 4:12-16. Paul expresses appreciation for his traveling companion, Ephaphras, who worked not only in his native Colossae, but also in Hierapolis and Laodicea. He asks the Colossians to greet the church in Laodicea, especially a woman named Nympha in whose house the church of Laodicea meets. And he instructs the Colossians to send his letter to them on to Laodicea and to "read also the letter [forwarded to Colossae] from Laodicea." Scholars speculate this last circulating letter was Paul's epistle to the Ephesians.

While Hierapolis is the major tourist destination today, Colossae was the first of the tri-cities to thrive, mostly due to the pure cold drinking water found there. At the time of Revelation's writing, location made Laodicea the greatest of the three. The north-south road from Sardis to the Mediterranean Sea and the east-west road from Ephesus to the Euphrates River crossed in the city's center.

Founded by the Seleucid King Antiochus II and named for his first wife, Laodice (prior to their separation in 253 BCE and her poisoning him seven years later), the city came under the control of Eumenes II of Pergamum in 188 BCE. Not surprisingly, the two primary gods of the capital city, Zeus and Asclepios, were worshipped in Laodicea. Along with Pergamum, Attalus III bequeathed Laodicea to the Romans in 133 BCE.

The Roman orator Cicero lived briefly in Laodicea, governing from 51-50 BCE. Hating the assignment, he laments in a letter penned four days after arrival:

I got to Laodicea on July 31. Notch up the days of my year of office from that date. I received as warm and enthusiastic a welcome as could be; but it's incredible how bored I am with the whole business, what inadequate scope I have for my well-known mental drive, and how unproductive my famous energy has become. Good God! Am I to sit in the courthouse at Laodicea while Aulus Plotius sits at Rome? And when our friend Caesar has that huge army, am I to have merely a couple of skeleton legions to my credit? In any case, those are not the things I want. The big world, the public stage, the Metropolis, my home, all of you – that is what I want![54]

Evidently the Risen Christ wasn't the only one ready to spit this city out of his mouth!

Laodicea was not a center for the imperial cult at the time of Revelation's writing and would not be awarded a temple until the reign of Emperor Commodus (180-192 CE). Emperor Tiberias turned down an earlier application, considering the city too poor to support the project – an understandable conclusion given the financial bailout he provided to rebuild its economy following the earthquake of 17 CE. No doubt the mission of the Roman legions stationed there after the earthquake included patrolling the two major commercial roads and protecting an economy rebuilt on three major industries: banking, wool, and pharmaceuticals.

Tiberias' stimulus package sparked significant wealth accumulation. When an earthquake struck again in 60 CE, despite offers of financial help from the Roman government, the citizens rebuilt *ek ton idion* – "from their own personal resources" – a phrase chiseled on marble plaques proudly displayed throughout the city at the time of Revelation's writing.

In 79 CE someone named Nicostratus gave the money to build a stadium, with continuous seating, nine hundred feet in length, the longest in Asia. A citizen named Pomponius Flaccus donated funds for heating the covered walks and for piping oil to the baths. Still another benefactor provided resources for the triple gate and towers erected between 88-90 CE.

The Risen Christ instructs John to write to the angel of the church in this highly affluent, self-sufficient, newly rebuilt, prideful city of Laodicea: "The words of the amen, the faithful and true witness, the sovereign of God's creation."

---

[54] Wilkinson, L. P. *Letters of Cicero.* New York: W.W. Norton, 1968. Pages 79-80. Quoted in Yamauchi, Edwin M. *New Testament Cities in Western Asia Minor.* Eugene, Oregon: Wipf and Stock Publishers, 1980. Pages 137-139.

In each of the first five letters, the titles for the Risen Christ are drawn from John's vision recorded in Revelation 1. While the second title, "faithful witness," is in the first chapter, both "the amen" and "the sovereign of God's creation" are not. Full understanding of the three titles, particularly the first and third, requires digging.

In the gospels, John uniquely uses the words "Verily, verily...," "Truly, truly...," or "Very truly..." to emphasize Jesus' sayings. The Greek translated in these various ways is "Amen. Amen..." Given that stylistic pattern, some argue John opens the letter to the seventh church with "Thus saith the amen" to signal the Laodiceans that what follows is the truth.

More likely is that Laodicean ears perked up because "the amen" is a title for God found only once in Hebrew scripture, Isaiah 65:16, a passage with obvious parallels to the rebuilding program underway in their city. Proclaims Isaiah:

> Then whoever invokes a blessing in the land
>   shall bless by the God of the amen,
> and whoever takes an oath in the land
>   shall swear by the God of the amen...

Modern translations substitute "the God of faithfulness" for "the God of the amen," causing some commentators to conclude "the amen" is no more than a redundant synonym for "faithful witness." But the prophetic context suggests more.

When the people of God return from exile, what their eyes behold brings lament to their lips. Isaiah 64:10-11 describes the scene:

> Zion has become a wilderness,
>   Jerusalem a desolation.
> Our holy and beautiful house,
>   where our ancestors praised you,
> has been burned by fire,
>   and all our pleasant places have become ruins.

Easily imaginable is Laodicea after the earthquake – homes destroyed, businesses wrecked, sanctuaries toppled.

In Isaiah 65, God responds by reminding the exiles that God has been waiting for their return, their turning around, their coming home to God – that is to say, for their repenting. God has been calling out to them continually, saying "Here I am, here I am..." But they have persisted in living as "a rebellious people, who walk in a way that is not good, following their own devices."

Their specific sin? According to Isaiah, they have participated in nature cults, engaged in pagan worship, taken part in séances, sought visions at various shrines, and eaten forbidden foods. Put succinctly, they have practiced idolatry. They have worshipped other gods.

Isaiah then names the sin even more precisely. The judgment of God falls, he proclaims, upon "you who forsake the Lord, who forget my holy mountain, who set a table for Fortune and fill cups of mixed wine for Destiny." Note the capitalization of "Fortune" and "Destiny" in Isaiah 65:11. These are not common nouns but the proper names of two gods – Gad and Meni – the Syrian gods of fortune and destiny, affluence and wealth, fate and luck.

In the panoply of Greek gods, Tyche was the one to whom mortals turned for such blessings. One of Tyche's three symbols was the cornucopia. The coins of Laodicea bore cornucopias.

Clearly the gods against whom Isaiah rails, the goddess whom the Laodiceans credit for their prosperity, the false diety of whatever name which lures people into believing they don't really need God, not when life is good, not when they have resources to do what they please, not when they need look nowhere beyond themselves to supply their needs – that god is the false god the Risen Christ confronts in the seventh letter.

The meaning of the title "Faithful and True Witness" appears self-evident. The Risen Christ stands in stark contrast to the unfaithful and untrue witness of the Laodicean church, seduced by material prosperity into comfortable complacency.

But the impact of the third title is not felt fully until we recognize the Laodiceans immediately would have linked "sovereign of God's creation" with Paul's letter to the Colossians, wherein the missionary describes the Cosmic Christ as present in the beginning of creation.

Paul opens by assuring the Colossians they are in his prayers. He knows "their faith in Christ Jesus," their "love...for all the saints," their "hope laid up...in heaven." That hope, he notes, is based on "the word of truth" which is "bearing fruit and growing" throughout the world, and especially in them. He prays they will "be filled with the knowledge of God's will," so that they "may lead lives worthy of the Lord."

Given the proximity and relatedness of the tri-cities, it is easy to imagine the Laodicean church anticipating a similar complimentary word in the letter it receives from John. Faith, hope, love, truth, fruit, knowledge, the leading of worthy lives – surely, from the Laodicean point of view, such terms apply every bit, if not more so, to them. But that is not the case – not from the vantage point of the Risen Christ.

In verses 15-20 of Colossians 1, Paul describes the Cosmic Christ as:

> ...the image of the invisible God, the first born of all creation; for in him all things in heaven and on earth were created, things visible and invisible, whether thrones or dominions or rulers or powers – all things have been created through him and for him. He himself is before all things, and in him all things hold together. He is the head of the body, the church; he is the beginning, the firstborn from the dead, so that he might come to have first place in everything. For in him all the fullness of God was pleased to dwell...

Paul's portrayal of the Cosmic Christ reinforces John's depiction of the Risen Christ. The "image of the invisible God" is the one "worthy to sit on the throne." To be given a word from his lips is to be addressed by no one less than God.

Either "first" or "source" or "head" or "origin" or "beginning" or "cause" is the usual translation of the Greek word *arche* used both by Paul (Colossians 1:15) and by John (Revelation 3:14). Another translation is "ruler." Because Revelation emphasizes the dominion of the Risen Christ over all creation (all the churches, all other gods, all that was and is and ever will be), and because Hebrew scripture often puts human beings back into their place by reminding that God is the Creator and we are not (the classic example being the conclusion of Job), we prefer translating the term as "sovereign."

The Laodiceans may feel good about themselves, but now they are coming face-to-face with "the amen, the faithful and true witness, the sovereign of God's creation," who is about to render judgment upon their behavior:

> I know your works; you are neither cold nor hot. I wish that you were either cold or hot. So, because you are lukewarm, and neither cold nor hot, I am about to spit you out of my mouth.

While memorable, the judgment perplexes. We understand why a church that is hot, on fire, filled with God's Spirit, literally "boiling over" with life is worthy of praise. We belong to or would love to become members of such congregations. We associate a cold church with unfriendly and unwelcoming, empty and lifeless, lacking joy and awe. So why would the Risen Christ prefer a cold church over a lukewarm church where there might be a little something going on? Clearly John has a different connotation of "cold" in mind.

Remember the context. Among the tri-cities, Hierapolis enjoyed natural hot springs, believed to hold medicinal value. The hot springs of Hierapolis offered waters of healing. Colossae enjoyed natural cold springs for quenching the thirst and refreshing the body. The cold springs of Colossae offered water necessary for life. Laodicea had neither hot nor cold springs. The city enjoyed no natural source of water for much of the year, depending instead upon water from hot springs flowing from a distance through an aqueduct. By the time that water traveled just over four miles to Laodicea, it was lukewarm. Moreover it was full of salts intensified by evaporation. The ruins of the aqueduct still contain salt encrustation.

The ancients used lukewarm heavily-salted mineral water for the same reason we keep Syrup of Ipecac in our medicine cabinets. It makes people vomit. "Vomit" – not "spew" or "spit" – is the best translation of the Greek. A church which thinks of itself too highly, fooling itself about its own faithfulness, is a church that makes the Risen Christ puke.

"For you say, 'I am rich, I have prospered, and I need nothing,'" the Risen Christ continues. "You do not realize that you are wretched, pitiful, poor, blind, and naked."

In the Greek a definite pronoun is attached to the word "wretched." The Laodiceans are the wretched ones *par excellence*.[55] Not exactly the image their Chamber of Commerce wanted posted at the city limits! "Welcome to Laodicea – Home to THE Most Wretched Church on the Face of the Earth." Not only "wretched" but also "pitiful." Again, not the reputation sought by a community which accepted pity from no one after the earthquake, proudly rebuilding their city from the ground up *ek ton idion*. "Poor, blind, and naked" – the very thought offended Laodicean sensitivities, for the economic mix creating their prosperity was one part banking, one part eye pharmaceuticals, and one part high-end clothing – industries recognized worldwide.

Poor? Laodicea was a financial hub. With the north-south and the east-west trade routes meeting at the city's center, merchants displayed wares from all four points of the compass. Business in the bazaar was thriving. Strabo reports that when Cicero arrived in Laodicea from Rome, he encountered no trouble at all cashing his large letters of credit.

Blind? Near Laodicea was a school of medicine based upon the teachings of the Greek physician Herophilos (330-250 BCE), who believed compound diseases required compound treatments. According to Galen, the renown physician to the emperors in Rome and to the gladiators in Pergamum, Laodicea was the only source in the world for two medicines: a tablet made of Phrygian stone ground into powder and applied to the eyelids; and an

---

[55] Morris, Leon. *The Revelation of St. John*. Grand Rapids: William B. Eerdmans Publishing House, 1969. Page 83.

ointment made from an aromatic plant called the spice nard, thought to be effective in treating ailments of the ears. Not surprising, some coins found in Laodicea depict the caduceus of Asclepios, the god of healing. Curiously a few bear names of individual physicians.

Naked? Again according to Strabo, "The country around Laodicea breeds excellent sheep, remarkable not only for the softness of their wool in which they surpass the Milesian sheep, but for their dark or raven color. The Laodiceans derive a large part of their revenue from them."[56] The black woolen tunic manufactured in their factories, called a *trimita*, was so identified with Laodicea that Laodiceans were referred to as the *Trimitaria*.[57] The city was famous for weaving fashionable black woolen garments for lucrative export.

How dare anyone call them poor, blind, and naked? But not letting up for a moment, the Laodiceans are confronted with these additional truths: (1) that that which is most valuable cannot be bought with their money; (2) that God can see right through their pretenses; and (3) that there are ailments which cannot be healed by their physicians.

"Therefore I counsel you, buy from me gold refined by fire so that you may be rich; and white robes to clothe you and to keep the shame of your nakedness from being seen; and salve to anoint your eyes so that you may see," declares the Risen Christ. "I reprove and discipline those whom I love."

If that sounds like tough love, it is. No words minced. No edge dulled. No blow softened. "Revelation is designed to unmask false senses of security," observes Craig Koester, Professor of New Testament at Luther Seminary in St. Paul, even "while beckoning readers to join the heavenly host in singing praises to God and the Lamb."[58]

"Be eager, therefore, and repent," the Risen Christ continues. The verb "repent" is an aorist imperative, indicating a specific action at a particular point in time. The verb "eager" is in the present imperative, denoting continuing activity. The sense of the command is this: "Make your decision. Make it now. Then never again let your drive to be faithful fail."

"Listen! I am standing at the door, knocking; if you hear my voice and open the door, I will come in to you and dine with you, and you with me." Holman Hunt made this line famous in his painting of Christ knocking, and knocking, and knocking on a door that only could be opened from the inside.

---

[56] Quoted in Barclay. Page 112.

[57] Cimok. Page 93.

[58] Koester, Craig R. *Revelation and the End of All Things*. Grand Rapids: William B. Eerdmans Publishing Company, 2001. Page 39f.

The promise to the Laodiceans is that if they finally let him in, the Risen Christ will dine with them. Not breakfast (seldom more than a piece of bread dipped in wine), nor lunch (a quick bite in the city square), but dinner (*deipnon*) – the long leisurely main meal at the end of the day when friends and family sit and talk for the work is done.[59]

Even more, the promise of the Risen Christ "To the one who conquers [is that] I will give a place with me on my throne, just as I myself conquered and sat down with my father on his throne." What greater gift could Christ offer in exchange for faithfulness?

Let anyone who has an ear listen
to what the Spirit is saying
to the churches.

---

[59] Barclay. Pages 120f.

10 "WHAT THE SPIRIT IS SAYING..."

The Dow Jones Industrial Average hit its all time high of 14,164 on October 9, 2007. Five years of climbing stock prices had caused more than one small investor to contemplate early retirement...including me. Then came the bear. Under the weight of subprime mortgages, the real estate bubble burst and the financial sector tanked. Continually falling over the next seventeen months, the Dow bottomed out on March 9, 2009 at 6547, having lost of 53.8% of its value.

Businesses laid off workers or closed up shop, causing unemployment to climb to nearly 10%. Businesses believed too big to fail – or to be allowed to fail – filed for bankruptcy, were bought up for pennies on the dollar, or received bail out money from the government. General Motors, the country's largest company, was dubbed "Government Motors" by pundits opposed to the trillions of dollars pumped into the economy by the Obama administration.

For creating unsound mortgage instruments to extend credit at unsustainable levels, lending institutions were deemed the primary culprit. But there was plenty of blame to go around. As Gary Dorrien, Union Theological Seminary's Professor of Social Ethics, sums it:

> Speculators gamed the system and regulators looked the other way. Mortgage brokers sold bad mortgages; bond bundlers packaged the loans into securities; rating agencies gave inflated bond ratings to the loans; corporate executives put the bonds on

their balance sheets; and all made fortunes off toxic products they had no business creating or passing off.[60]

Wall Street was not the only tumbling market. Other governments also acted in the hope of stabilizing a rapidly down-spinning global economy.

In the same way that I did not believe the terrorist attack of 9-11 marked the beginning of Armageddon, I do not believe the largest financial crisis since the Great Depression is a sign of the end-times. But I do believe it exposes the fact that the citizens of the United States are living in an empire – what David Ray Griffin (Professor Emeritus of Philosophy and Theology at Claremont School of Theology) and others are calling "the world's first borderless empire."[61]

The word "empire" has returned to the American vocabulary after decades of silence. Griffin notes that people spoke freely in the nineteenth century of the creation of an "American Empire," a "benign, even a benevolent, empire," an "empire of liberty." But, he argues, by the twentieth century "the negative connotations of the word 'imperialism'…[had] spread to the word 'empire,' so that at the very time the United States was creating the most extensive empire the world had ever known, politicians and respectable intellectuals had to deny that there *was* an American empire." Now, in the early part of the twenty-first century, the word is regaining acceptance under the myth that the United States only extends its influence and flexes its muscle for the noble purpose of promoting democracy – not the baser motive of wealth accumulation.[62]

Given that the American colonies so chaffed under the rule of the British Empire that they waged war to win independence, for there to have been conversations in the late 1700s and early 1800s about the creation of an alternative kind of empire is understandable. But history records what actually happened next was a westward expansion of the newly formed nation, in which additional land was claimed, purchased for a pittance, or taken by military force under the imperial rubric of manifest destiny.

Embracing the industrial revolution and blessed with raw materials, the United States looked beyond its borders for cheap labor and ready markets.

---

[60] Quoted in "The Kairos in this Collapse," *Balaam's Courier.* 27th United Church of Christ General Synod, June 26, 2009. Page 6.

[61] Griffin, David Ray and others. *The American Empire and the Commonwealth of God: A Political, Economic, Religious Statement.* Louisville: Westminster John Knox Press, 2006. Page v.

[62] Griffin and others. Page 3.

Without creating formal colonies, the country took advantage of unequal political clout, economic leverage, and military prowess to satisfy its insatiable appetite, even to the point of human enslavement. "We shall not make Britain's mistake," declared the business tycoon Ludwell Denny in 1930; "too wise to try to govern the world, we shall merely own it."[63] Ironically, the burdening of poor countries with huge debt in order to enrich life in the United States is not unlike the oppression against which the original thirteen colonies rebelled.

In the United States "the pursuit of happiness" is considered an "inalienable right." However, happiness tends to be defined in individual economic terms, and it is pursued with too little concern for the cost to others. Never was this more clearly revealed than just before the United Nations 1992 Earth Summit in Rio de Janeiro, when the first President Bush decreed that "the American way of life is not negotiable." Writes Richard Falk, Professor of International Law and Practice at Princeton:

> This was itself a rather imperial expression of an incredible position – that although human survival might be endangered, the bloated American standard of living (and waste) would not be reduced. Such moral and political decadence with respect to human destiny has rarely been so openly embraced.[64]

From John's prophetic point-of-view, the American way of life has become the primary god in our empire. John would call upon the citizens of the United States – particularly those in churches – to repent and resist. John would pronounce God's judgment upon our arrogant greed. In the language of the apocalyptic genre, John would translate the anxiety accompanying the current financial crisis into dire wails of anguishing lament, not unlike Revelation 18.

That chapter vividly portrays those in grief at the funeral of the Babylonian, the Roman, the American way of life. There are three groups of mourners – monarchs, merchants, and mariners. The sovereigns of other nations, who have prospered through their close relationship with the world's only superpower, stand at a distance fearing the same judgment might befall them. The sellers weep "since no one buys their merchandise anymore." What follows next in the text sounds like a cargo ship's inventory:

---

[63] Griffin and others. Page 3.

[64] Griffin and others. Page 57.

gold and silver
jewels and pearls,
fine linen, purple,
silk and scarlet,
all kinds of scented wood,
all articles of ivory,
all articles of costly wood, bronze, iron, and marble,
cinnamon, spice, incense, myrrh, frankincense,
wine, olive oil, choice flour and wheat,
cattle and sheep,
horses and chariots,
slaves, and...

Don't read quickly over the final item on board:

the souls of human beings.

Concludes John, "The fruits that your soul lusted after are gone..." In an hour – in no time at all – everything is gone. Cry out "all shipmasters and seafarers, sailors and all whose trade is on the sea... 'Alas, alas, the great city, where all who had ships at sea grew rich by her wealth...has been laid waste.'"

In the genre of apocalyptic literature, the purpose of such a vision is to toll the death bell on a way of life that is not of God. Its function is to extend an invitation to heed the prophetic call to change, to repent, to "come out." Comments Craig Koester:

> The angel...refers to "the merchants of the earth" who have "grown rich from the power of her luxury" (18:3), but the Christians of Laodicea [for example] also fell into this category, for their primary source of security was wealth, not Christ (3:17). When the heavenly voice cries "Come out of her, my people" (18:4), it speaks especially to readers who are being lulled into complacency by their prosperity, or who find compromising the integrity of their faith to be a reasonable price to pay for the favors offered by the harlot [Rome]. The call to "Come out of her" echoes a similar plea by Jeremiah (Jer. 51:45)... The angelic voice beckons them to disassociate themselves from the infidelity and materialism that were the

hallmark of the great city's trade, following instead in the ways of the Lamb.[65]

But did the churches in Ephesus, Smyrna, Pergamum, Thyatira, Sardis, Philadelphia, and Laodicea have ears to hear?

Do we?

Each of the letters to the seven churches ends with the same exhortation: "Let anyone who has an ear listen to what the spirit is saying to the churches." Notice that the word "churches" is plural. While each church receives an individualized letter, the Risen Christ instructs every church to hear and appropriate the prophetic word delivered to the others. Accordingly, it is a mistake to read the seven letters today and ask: "Which ancient church is most like ours?" Experience teaching the letters confirms that congregants easily see something of themselves in all seven.

The call to have ears to hear the word of God alludes to the charge given Isaiah, later cited in Jesus' explanation of why he taught with parables.

In the sixth chapter of Isaiah, the eighth century BCE prophet, while worshipping in the Temple, receives a vision of God in the throne room (not unlike the vision John reports in the fourth and fifth chapters of Revelation). The heavenly court is singing God's praises: "Holy, holy, holy is the LORD of host; the whole earth is full of God's glory." Like Moses hiding his face in the cleft of the rock while the glory of God passes by, like John falling on his face upon glimpsing the Risen Christ, Isaiah recognizes immediately that no sinful human being can stand in the presence of God's holiness. So he confesses: "Woe is me…for I am a person of unclean lips, and I live among a people of unclean lips…" After granting Isaiah forgiveness, God asks: "Whom shall I send, and who will go for us?" Isaiah famously replies, "Here am I; send me!" Then God instructs Isaiah: "Go and say to this people:

> Keep listening, but do not comprehend;
>> keep looking, but do not understand.
> Make the mind of this people dull,
>> and stop their ears and shut their eyes,
> so that they may not look with their eyes
>> and listen with their ears,
> and comprehend with their minds,
>> and turn and be healed.

---

[65] Koester. Page 164.

The oracle is the opposite of what one expects, suggesting God does not want the people to hear and respond to God's will. But theological difficulties notwithstanding, from a literary point-of-view, the function of those verses is to explain why the inhabitants of Jerusalem pay no attention to Isaiah's attempts to prophesy to the religious, social, economic, political, and military life of Judah. Moreover, they lift up the reality that when it comes to hearing a prophetic word, hard-heartedness inevitably leads to deafness. As Jesus explains to his questioning disciples, "The reason I speak to them in parables is that 'seeing they do not perceive, and hearing they do not listen, nor do they understand.'" (Matthew 13:13).

Perhaps Revelation would be much less mysterious if John had chosen to write in parables instead of the apocalyptic genre! But this much is clear: John wants readers, in every church in every place in every time, to open up their ears and listen closely – really hear – what the Spirit of God is saying to all seven churches.

In the preceding chapters we have named some of the gods in the Roman province of Asia in the late first century which John perceives are staking their claim on the churches' devotion:

- In Ephesus: the god of vested economic interests, the god of governmental authority, and the god of self-righteous fundamentalism;

- In Smyrna: the god of patriotic nationalism, the god of the religious establishment, and the god of fear;

- In Pergamum: the god of military might, the god of medical healing, and the god of unfaithful compromise;

- In Thyatira: the god of indiscriminate toleration;

- In Sardis: the god of living in the past;

- In Philadelphia: the god of missional timidity; and

- In Laodicea: the god of wealth, the god of false security, and the god of prideful self-sufficiency.

In inviting us to listen to what the Spirit is saying, John is calling us to confront not only these specific gods but also all other contenders for God's throne and our devotion. John names the names of some of the principalities and powers at work in our world in order to call the church back to the God revealed in the Risen Christ. It is important for us to hear John's prophetic message today because Protestantism has done a disservice to the church by mistaking "the prophets' critique of idolatry – the false worship of gods – for a denial of their existence all together."[66] Writes Wink:

> ...the old gods of paganism are still very much alive... Hidden from consciousness, they strike from concealment and craze or cripple us without our having the slightest comprehension as to what has happened... The gods live. They are real but not ultimate, transcendent but not absolute, suprahuman but not superior to humans, more powerful than we yet subject to our responses...[67]

Born in St. Louis of a prominent family, the Nobel Prize winning poet T.S. Eliot attended private academies in New England before studying philosophy – particularly Buddhism and Hinduism – at Harvard and Oxford. Of ill health, in an ill-fated marriage, disillusioned by World War I, Eliot visited churches to admire their beauty and take solace in their quiet. To the surprise of his friends and family, on a visit to Rome he suddenly knelt before Michelangelo's *la Pieta* statue, with all the contriteness of one finally submitting to a higher authority. One year later he was baptized and published the first of what are called the *Ariel Poems* – a work entitled "Journey of the Magi."

Haunting in its retelling of the story of those mysterious figures from the East who followed a star until they found the Christ Child, the poem depicts their encounter with God as the most disturbing experience of their lives. "...Were we led all that way for Birth or Death?" they ask, for we "...had seen birth and death,/But had thought they were different; this Birth was/Hard and bitter agony for us, like Death, our death." Then writes the poet:

> ...We returned to our places, these Kingdoms,
> But no longer at ease here, in the old dispensation,
> With an alien people clutching their gods...

---

[66] Wink. *Unmasking the Powers.* Page 108.

[67] Wink. *Unmasking the Powers.* Pages 108, 127.

John pens a vision of the Risen Christ so that we will live "no longer at ease." Beginning with the letters to the seven churches and throughout the remaining chapters, John uses all the power of apocalyptic language to make the church uncomfortable. John believes God alone demands our full devotion. Asks John: what are the lesser gods to which we cling so dearly?

Let anyone who has an ear listen
to what the Spirit is saying
to the churches.

APPENDIX A: TOPOLOGICAL MAP

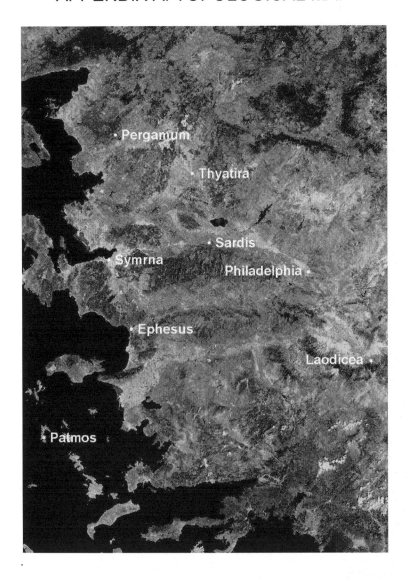

The original image can be found at http://visibleearth.nasa.gov/.
The original image has been cropped and the names added.
NASA owns the original image.

APPENDIX B: LETTERS BY SECTION

Each letter found in Revelation 2-3, with two exceptions, contains seven sections. This appendix contains the author's analysis.

	Greeting	Title	Praise	Criticism	Warning	Promise	Exhortation
Ephesus	2:1a	2:1b	2:2-3,6	2:4	2:5	2:7b	2:7a
Smyrna	2:8a	2:8b	2:9		2:10a	2:10b,11b	2:11a
Pergamum	2:12a	2:12b	2:13	2:14-15	2:16	2:17b	2:17a
Thyatira	2:18a	2:18b	2:19	2:20-21	2:22-23	2:24-28	2:29
Sardis	3:1a	3:1b	3:1c,4a	3:2	3:3	3:4b-5	3:6
Philadelphia	3:7a	3:7b	3:8		3:11	3:9-10,12	3:13
Laodicea	3:14a	3:14b		3:15-17	3:18-19	3:20-21	3:22

Greeting

Ephesus: *To the angel of the church in Ephesus write:*

Smyrna: *To the angel of the church in Smyrna write:*

Pergamum: *To the angel of the church in Pergamum write:*

Thyatira: *To the angel of the church in Thyatira write:*

Sardis: *To the angel of the church in Sardis write:*

Philadelphia: *To the angel of the church in Philadelphia write:*

Laodicea: *To the angel of the church in Laodicea write:*

Title

Ephesus: *These are the words of him who holds the seven stars in his right hand, who walks among the seven golden lamp stands:*

Smyrna: *These are the words of the first and the last, who was dead and came to life:*

Pergamum: *These are the words of him who has the sharp two-edged sword:*

Thyatira: *These are the words of the Son of God, who has eyes like a flame of fire, and whose feet are like burnished bronze:*

Sardis: *These are the words of him who has the seven spirits of God and the seven stars:*

Philadelphia: *These are the words of the holy one, the true one, who has the key of David, who opens and no one will shut, who shuts and no one opens:*

Laodicea: [These are] *the words of the Amen, the faithful and true witness, the origin of God's creation:*

Praise

Ephesus: *I know your works, your toil and your patient endurance. I know that you cannot tolerate evildoers; you have tested those who claim to be apostles but are not, and have found them to be false. I also know that you are enduring patiently and bearing up for the sake of my name, and that you have not grown weary... Yet this is to your credit: you hate the works of the Nicolaitans, which I also hate.*

Smyrna: *I know your affliction and your poverty, even though you are rich. I know the slander on the part of those who say that they are Jews and are not, but are a synagogue of Satan.*

Pergamum: *I know where you are living, where Satan's throne is. Yet you are holding fast to my name, and you did not deny your faith in me even in the days of Antipas my witness, my faithful one, who was killed among you, where Satan lives.*

Thyatira: *I know your works — your love, faith, service, and patient endurance. I know that your last works are greater than the first.*

Sardis: *I know your works. You have a name of being alive, but you are dead... Yet you have still a few persons in Sardis who have not soiled their clothes;*

Philadelphia: *I know your works. Look, I have set before you an open door, which no one is able to shut. I know that you have but little power, and yet you have kept my word and have not denied my name.*

Laodicea:

Criticism

Ephesus: *But I have this against you: that you have abandoned the love you had at first.*

Smyrna:

Pergamum: *But I have a few things against you: you have some there who hold to the teaching of Balaam, who taught Balak to put a stumbling block before the people of Israel, so that they would eat food sacrificed to idols and practice fornication. So you also have some who hold to the teaching of the Nicolaitans.*

Thyatira: *But I have this against you: you tolerate that woman Jezebel, who calls herself a prophet and is teaching and beguiling my servants to practice fornication and to eat food sacrificed to idols. I gave her time to repent, but she refuses to repent of her fornication.*

Sardis: *Wake up, and strengthen what remains and is on the point of death, for I have not found your works perfect in the sight of my God.*

Philadelphia:

Laodicea: *I know your works; you are neither cold nor hot. I wish that you were either cold or hot. So, because you are lukewarm, and neither cold nor hot, I am about to spit you out of my mouth. For you say, "I am rich, I have prospered, and I need nothing." You do not realize that you are wretched, pitiable, poor, blind, and naked.*

Warning

Ephesus: *Remember then from what you have fallen, repent, and do the works you did at first. If not, I will come to you and remove your lamp stand from its place, unless you repent.*

Smyrna: *Do not fear what you are about to suffer. Beware, the devil is about to throw some of you into prison so that you may be tested, and for ten days you will have affliction.*

Pergamum: *Repent then. If not, I will come to you soon and make war against them with the sword of my mouth.*

Thyatira: *Beware, I am throwing her on a bed, and those who commit adultery with her I am throwing into great distress, unless they repent of her doings; and I will strike her children dead. And all the churches will know that I am the one who searches minds and hearts, and I will give to each of you as your works deserve.*

Sardis: *Remember then what you received and heard; obey it, and repent. If you do not wake up, I will come like a thief, and you will not know at what hour I will come to you.*

Philadelphia: *I am coming soon; hold fast to what you have, so that no one may seize your crown.*

Laodicea: *Therefore I counsel you to buy from me gold refined by fire so that you may be rich; and white robes to clothe you and to keep the shame of your nakedness from being seen; and salve to anoint your eyes so that you may see. I reprove and discipline those whom I love. Be earnest, therefore, and repent.*

Promise

Ephesus: *To everyone who conquers I will give permission to eat from the tree of life that is in the paradise of God.*

Smyrna: *Be faithful until death and I will give you the crown of life... Whoever conquers will not be harmed by the second death.*

Pergamum: *To everyone who conquers I will give some of the hidden manna, and I will give a white stone, and on the white stone is written a new name that no one knows except the one who receives it.*

Thyatira: *But to the rest of you in Thyatira, who do not hold this teaching, who have not learned what some call 'the deep things of Satan,' to you I say, I do not lay on you any other burden; only hold fast to what you have until I come. To everyone who conquers and continues to do my works to the end, I will give authority over the nations; to rule them with an iron rod, as when clay pots are shattered – even as I also received authority from my father. To the one who conquers I will also give the morning star.*

Sardis: *They will walk with me, dressed in white, for they are worthy. If you conquer, you will be clothed like them in white robes, and I will not blot your name out of the book of life; I will confess your name before my father and before his angels.*

Philadelphia: *I will make those of the synagogue of Satan who say that they are Jews and are not, but are lying – I will make them come and bow down before your feet, and they will learn that I have loved you. Because you have kept my word of patient endurance, I will keep you from the hour of trial that is coming on the whole world to test the inhabitants of the earth... If you conquer, I will make you a pillar in the temple of my God; you will never go out of it. I will write on you the name of my God, and the name of the city of my God, the new Jerusalem that comes down from my God out of heaven, and my own new name.*

Laodicea: *Listen! I am standing at the door, knocking; if you hear my voice and open the door, I will come in to you and eat with you, and you with me. To the one who conquers I will give a place with me on my throne, just as I myself conquered and sat down with my father on his throne.*

Exhortation

Ephesus: *Let anyone who has an ear listen to what the Spirit is saying to the churches.*

Smyrna: *Let anyone who has an ear listen to what the Spirit is saying to the churches.*

Pergamum: *Let anyone who has an ear listen to what the Spirit is saying to the churches.*

Thyatira: *Let anyone who has an ear listen to what the Spirit is saying to the churches.*

Sardis: *Let anyone who has an ear listen to what the Spirit is saying to the churches.*

Philadelphia: *Let anyone who has an ear listen to what the Spirit is saying to the churches.*

Laodicea: *Let anyone who has an ear listen to what the Spirit is saying to the churches.*

APPENDIX C: WORSHIP RESOURCES

Asked to preach a series of sermons on the letters to the seven churches, the author selected texts from the Hebrew scriptures to be read along with the passages from Revelation; chose opening, sermon, and closing hymns inspired by the last book in the Bible; and composed prayers of confession based on the lesson. These resources are offered for your use either in corporate worship, small group devotions accompanying class discussions, or personal meditation. The hymns may be found in *The New Century Hymnal* (Cleveland: The Pilgrim Press, 1995.) Permission is granted to reprint the prayers.

Ephesus

Hebrew Scripture: Deuteronomy 6:4-9

Greek Scripture: Revelation 2:1-7

Hymns: *God Is Truly With Us*
What Wondrous Love Is This
Come, We Who Love God's Name

Prayer: Almighty, all-knowing, ever-loving God: you hold the universe, the entire world, the church on earth and in heaven, each and every one of us in the palm of your hand. Have mercy on us, for we confess before you our failures in love. You call us to love you with all our heart, soul, strength and mind. You call us to love our neighbors as we love ourselves. You call us to love our enemies. But we have not done so. Forgive us. Increase our love until it is as steadfast as your own. For we pray in the name of him whose love was so great that he laid down his very life for our sake…

Smyrna

Hebrew Scripture: Isaiah 44:6-8

Greek Scripture: Revelation 2:8-11

Hymns: *Holy God We Praise Your Name*
Savior God Above
My Hope Is Built on Nothing Less

Prayer: O God: You are the alpha and the omega, the beginning and the end, the only true God. Hear our prayer. We confess to you and before one another our failures in faith. In the face of powers greater than ourselves, we have cowered. Under the weight of too much pressure, we have bowed. Made rich by too many things, our souls have become impoverished. Cast away our fears and strengthen our resolve to stand tall as your witnesses. For we pray this in the name of him who has never done us wrong, who has promised us new life, who has brought resurrection to light...

Pergamum

Hebrew Scripture: Micah 6:3-8

Greek Scripture: Revelation 2:12-17

Hymns: *Holy, Holy, Holy*
Where Cross the Crowded Ways of Life
Guide Me, O My Great Redeemer

Prayer: In your glory, O Risen One, you sit on the throne. Before you are gathered all the peoples of the world. With your sharp two-edged sword, yours is the final authority separating the sheep from the goats, the good from the evil, the saved from the punished. Forgive us, we pray. Take mercy upon our country. No one needs to set temptation as a stumbling block in our path, for we surround ourselves with occasions to sin. With your grace, help us put an end to our hurtful ways. Save us from the sickness of our own sinfulness. Grant us healing, so that we may join you in bringing healing to the nations…

Thyatira

Hebrew Scripture: First Kings 16:29-33

Greek Scripture: Revelation 2:18-29

Hymns: *The God of Abraham Praise*
                         Jesus, Keep Me Near the Cross
                         Jesus Shall Reign

Prayer: All-knowing God, you sent your son into the world, not to condemn the world, but to save it. Yet, because he comes into our lives knowing our every thought, our every word, our every deed, we look up and see the lightening flash of his eyes. Forgive us, we pray. We confess to having tolerated evil instead of overcoming it with good. We repent of having drunk deeply from wells not filled with living water. Do not give us what we deserve. In your mercy, let us look up and see in your eyes the grace of the new morning star. . .

Sardis

Hebrew Scripture: Daniel 12:1-3

Greek Scripture: Revelation 3:1-6

Hymns: *You Servants of God, Your Sovereign Proclaim*
I Want to Be Ready
All Hail the Power of Jesus' Name

Prayer: You, O God, are worthy to receive all blessing and honor and glory and power, wisdom and riches and strength evermore. We are not. Bearing the name "Christian," we nevertheless sleepwalk through life, going through the motions of following your son, unaware of how our ways remain those of the world. Startle us out of our daydreams. Shake us when we drift off. Stir us up so we become conscious of our higher calling, fully awake to the new life you offer both in this world and in the world to come. . .

Philadelphia

Hebrew Scripture: Isaiah 22:20-25

Greek Scripture: Revelation 3:7-13

Hymns: *Rejoice, Give Thanks, and Sing*
Blessed Assurance
Crown With Your Richest Crowns

Prayer: All-powerful and all-knowing God: we bring before you those moments in our lives when we have not been up to the task, when we have fallen short of both our best intentions and your divine will. Though we have tried to be faithful disciples who stand up to evil, unexpected stuff happens, unintended consequences spring out of control, events in life overwhelm, leaving us feeling small, alone, inadequate, even trapped. Forgive our doubting of your presence, your caring, and your ultimate victory. When we face the tougher times, strengthen us...

Laodicea

Hebrew Scripture: Hosea 12:2-9

Greek Scripture: Revelation 3:14-22

Hymns: *Lift High the Cross*
Shall We Gather at the River
Unite and Join Your Cheerful Songs

Prayer: O God: you know how we hate being deceived by others, and we know we are not to deceive others. Yet if truth be known, our most common sin is our own self-deception. You know our airs and pretenses. You know our blind spots and cover-ups. You know our excuses and rationalizations. You know what we cannot face and refuse to admit. Yet you still stand at the door of our lives and keep knocking...and knocking...and knocking. In this moment of prayer, we open that door, letting the light of your truth reveal our need. . .

APPENDIX D: DISCUSSION QUESTIONS

"To the Angel of the Church..."

1. How would you describe the angel of your church?
2. How would non-attending residents of the area where you live describe your church?
3. If the Risen Christ dictated a letter to your church, what would it say?

Ephesus

1. What vested interests claim a stake on your life?
2. What actions of our government appear to be in conflict with Christian faith?
3. What is your experience of and reaction to religious fundamentalism?

Smyrna

1. What aspect of your church needs to move from death to life?
2. What pressures do you feel as Christians in America today?
3. What fears silence your witness?

Pergamum

1. How would you characterize evil?
2. Where do you draw the line with compromise?
3. What social justice issues need confronting where you live?

Thyatira

1. How does you church handle internal conflict?
2. What has your church tolerated long enough?
3. What is your church doing right that you need to hold fast?

Sardis

1. What is the reputation of your church?
2. Does your church spend more time looking backwards or forward?
3. What wake-up call needs sounding in your church?

Philadelphia

1. What is your church's mission?
2. When has faith in God helped your church through a troubled time?
3. What priority has evangelism in your church?

Laodicea

1. How would you describe the relationship between your church and the wider church?
2. What is the difference between healthy self-esteem and sinful pride?
3. To what do you look for security?

"What the Spirit is Saying…"

1. What are the marks of an empire?
2. What parallels do you perceive between ancient Rome and the United States of America?
3. What is the Spirit saying to your church in these times?

BIBLIOGRAPHY

Regarding the Seven Churches and Cities

_____. *Patmos: The Holy Island of the Apocalypse.* Attiki: Michalis Toubis S.A., 2006.

Aksit, Ilhan. *Pamukkale: Hierapolis.* Istanbul: Aksit Kultur Turizm Sanat Ajans Ltd. Sti., 2001.

Barclay, William. *Letters to the Seven Churches.* Philadelphia: The Westminster Press, 1957.

Blake, Everett C. & Anna G. Edmonds. *Biblical Sites in Turkey.* Istanbul: SEV Matbaacilik ve Yayincilik, 1997.

Cimok, Fatih. *A Guide to the Seven Churches.* Istanbul: A Turizm Yayinlari Ltd, 1998.

Cimok, Fatih. *Pergamum.* Istanbul: A Turism Yayinlari, 2001.

Hemer, Colin J. *The Letters to the Seven Churches of Asia in Their Local Setting.* Grand Rapids: William B. Eerdmans Publishing Company, 1989.

Erdemgil, Shelahattin. *Ephesus.* Istanbul: Net Turistik Yayinlar A.S., 2006.

Ramsay, William. *The Letters to the Seven Churches.* Reprinted by Grand Rapids: Baker Book House, 1985 from the 1904 Edition published by Hodder and Stoughton, London.

Von Zabern, Philipp. *The Pergamon Altar.* Mainz am Rhein: Staatliche Museen zu Berlin, 1995.

Worth, Roland H., Jr. *The Seven Cities of the Apocalypse and Greco-Asian Culture.* New York: Paulist Press, 1999.

Worth, Roland H., Jr. *The Seven Cities of the Apocalypse and Roman Culture.* New York: Paulist Press, 1999.

Yamauchi, Edwin M. *New Testament Cities in Western Asia Minor: Light from Archaeology on Cities of Paul and the Seven Churches of Revelation.* Eugene, Oregon: Wipf & Stock Publishers, 1980.

Regarding the Book of Revelation in Its Entirety

Barclay, William. *The Revelation of John* (Volume 1). Philadelphia: The Westminster Press, 1976.

Berrigan, Daniel. *The Nightmare of God.* Portland: Sunburst Press, 1983.

Blevins, James L. *Revelation.* Atlanta: John Knox Press, 1984.

Boesak, Allan A. *Comfort and Protest: The Apocalypse from a South-African Perspective.* Philadelphia: The Westminster Press, 1987.

Boring, M. Eugene. *Revelation (Interpretation: A Bible Commentary for Teaching and Preaching).* Louisville: John Knox Press, 1989.

Fiorenza, Elisabath Schüssler. *The Book of Revelation: Justice and Judgment.* Minneapolis: Fortress Press, 1998.

Fiorenza, Elisabeth Schüssler. *Revelation: Vision of a Just World* (Gerhard Krodel, Ed. *Proclamation Commentaries*). Minneapolis: Fortress Press, 1991.

Gonzalez, Catherine Gunsalus and Justo L. Gonzalez. *Revelation* (Patrick D. Miller and David L Bartlett, Eds. *Westminster Bible Companion*). Louisville: Westminster John Knox Press, 1997.

Keller, Catherine. *Apocalypse Now and Then: A Feminist Guide to the End of the World.* Boston: Beacon Press, 1996.

Koester, *Craig R. Revelation and the End of All Things*, Grand Rapids: William B. Eerdmans Publishing Company, 2001.

Koester, Craig R. *Is This the Time? Interpreting the Mystery of Revelation* (DVD with CD-ROM Study Guide). St. Paul: Luther Productions, 2003.

Kraybill, J. Nelson. *Apocalypse and Allegiance: Worship, Politics, and Devotion in the Book of Revelation.* Grand Rapids: Brazos Press, 2010.

Maier, Harry O. *Apocalypse Recalled: The Book of Revelation after Christendom.* Minneapolis: Fortress Press, 2002.

Metzger, Bruce M. *Breaking the Code: Understanding the Book of Revelation.* Nashville: Abingdon Press, 1993.

Morris, Leon. *The Revelation of St. John.* Grand Rapids: William B. Eerdmans Publishing House, 1969.

Thompson, Leonard L. *Revelation* (Victor Paul Furnish, Ed. *Abingdon New Testament Commentaries*). Nashville: Abingdon Press, 1998.

Thompson, Leonard L. *The Book of Revelation: Apocalypse and Empire.* New York: Oxford University Press, 1990.

Vidal, Kim S. *Moon Under Her Feet: Women of the Apocalypse.* Cleveland: The Pilgrim Press, 2001.

Additional Consulted Works

_____. *Revelation as a Critique of Empire, Interpretation: A Journal of Bible and Theology.* Volume 63. Number 1, January 2009.

Borg, Marcus J. *Reading the Bible Again for the First Time: Taking the Bible Seriously but Not Literally.* New York: Harper-Collins Publishers, Inc., 2001.

Borg, Marcus J. and John Dominic Crossan. *The First Christmas: What the Gospels Really Teach About Jesus's Birth.* New York: HarperOne, 2007.

Burkert, Walter. *Greek Religion.* Cambridge: Harvard University Press, 1985.

Kleist, James A. *The Didache, The Epistle of Barnabas, The Epistles and the Martyrdom of St. Polycarp, The Fragments of Papias, The Epistle to Diognetus* (Johannes Quasten and Joseph C. Plumpe, Eds. *Ancient Christian Writers*, Volume 6). New York: The Newman Press, 1948.

Osborn, Kevin and Dana L. Burgess. *The Complete Idiot's Guide to Classical Mythology.* Second Edition. New York: Penguin Group, 2004.

Wink, Walter. *Engaging the Powers: Discernment and Resistance in a World of Domination.* Minneapolis: Fortress Press, 1992.

Wink, Walter. *Naming the Powers: The Language of Power in the New Testament.* Philadelphia: Fortress Press, 1984.

Wink, Walter. *The Powers That Be: Theology for a New Millennium.* New York: Random House, 1998.

Wink, Walter. *Unmasking the Powers: The Invisible Forces That Determine Human Existence.* Philadelphia: Fortress Press, 1986.

Pertinent Reference Books

_____. *The Museum of Anatolian Civilizations.* Ankara: Donmez Offset Muze Eserleri Turistik Yayinlari, copyrighted without year indicated.

Aland, Kurt and others. *The Greek New Testament* (Second Edition). Stuttgart: United Bible Societies, 1968.

Freedman, David Noel (Editor-in-Chief). *The Anchor Bible Dictionary.* New York: Doubleday, 1992.

Kittel, Gerhard. *Theological Dictionary of the New Testament.* Grand Rapids: Wm. B. Eerdmans Publishing Co., 1964.

ABOUT THE AUTHOR

Kent Ulery served as the 10th President and Professor of Pastoral Leadership of Bangor Theological Seminary, having previously served for 21 years as a local church pastor in Indiana, Illinois, and Michigan, as well as 12 years as the Conference Minister for the Michigan Conference of the United Church of Christ.

Ulery received his Bachelor of Arts from DePauw University, where he majored in New Testament and was inducted into Phi Beta Kappa. His Master of Divinity was earned at Princeton Theological Seminary, where he concentrated in New Testament studies. His Doctor of Ministry degree was awarded by McCormick Theological Seminary in the area of Parish Revitalization.

He and his wife, Meg, live in Arlington Heights, Illinois. They have two sons and daughters-in-law living near Atlanta and Chicago. Together they find great joy playing with their grandchildren.

Isaia - 64 & 65 chap.
The Amen, the Trustworthy and True
witness,

Revelation - 16 -18
Revelation - 19
(hallelulah)

Emperor
Kings of the Earth
magnate, generals the rich
powerful
_____

skilled trades - teachers
peasants & poor
slaves & expendables

1. new revised standard Bible
č the apocalypse
2. common English Bible -

Made in the USA
Columbia, SC
24 March 2018